ON T

The wail pierced the darkness like a knife in the gut. It was the shriek of a woman, in agony.

Her screams sliced through the walls of a rural house sitting off Highway 49, and fell on the ears of Shirley and Rick McCloud and their son, Rick Jr., twenty-three. Opening the door, the McClouds found a young woman, wild-eyed and shaking.

"He's taken my kids in my car!" she blurted. "A black man has taken my kids and my car!"

At first, they could barely make out what the woman was saying.

"I was at a red light. This black man put a gun to my head and told me to drive. I asked him why he was doing this. He told me to shut up or he'd kill me."

The young woman said she drove around for miles with the gunman in the passenger seat, until he ordered her out of the car near the McCloud residence.

"Can I take my kids?" the mother told them she had pleaded.

"I don't have time to get them out of the car seats," was the man's curt reply.

By her account, the carjacker did, however, find time to promise that he wouldn't harm the children. As the man leaped into the driver's seat and sped off, she said, he left her standing along the highway, crying out to her lost boys.

"I love y'all!"

Mother Love, Deadly Love

THE SUSAN SMITH MURDERS

Andrea Peyser

HarperPaperbacks
A Division of HarperCollinsPublishers

For Mark

HarperPaperbacks *A Division of* HarperCollins*Publishers*
10 East 53rd Street, New York, N.Y. 10022

Cover photograph: Andy Burriss / The Rock Hill *Herald* / SYGMA
Inset cover photograph: American Fast Photo / SYGMA

First printing: March 1995

Printed in the United States of America

HarperPaperbacks and colophon are trademarks of HarperCollins*Publishers*

❖ 10 9 8 7 6 5 4 3 2 1

Acknowledgments

During the course of writing this book, I was fortunate to have known a great many wonderful people who offered their aid and inspiration, or who were simply generous enough to leave me alone when necessary. I am indebted to every one of you.

I would like to thank my cheerful slave drivers at the *New York Post*—Ken Chandler, Martin Singerman, John Cassidy, Marc Kalech, Steve Cuozzo, and Stuart Marques for giving me the time and encouragement to get through this.

Many thanks also to Laura Harris, the *Post*'s brilliant librarian, without whom this book might not have been possible. My gratitude to Gretchen Viehmann, assistant photo editor, for her invaluable help; to David Rentas, photojournalist extraordinaire; and Jeff Simmons, ace reporter, who has a standing offer to be my press agent.

I am especially grateful to my editor at Harper-Paperbacks, Jessica Lichtenstein, for her extraordinary patience and unfailing ability to talk me down from high places.

To my mother, Ruth Peyser, and my sister, Rhona Peyser, thanks for believing in me all these years.

Thanks to Frank L. Eppes, for his perspective.

I also must thank my red-headed gal pals, Susan Lisovicz and Sparkle Hayter, for just being there, somewhere; to Mary McGeary for her moral support; to Allison, Gregg, Aubrey, and Baby Doe Mallinger, just because; to Anne Bers; Maria and James Zappa Marshall; Laura Killroy; and to Dominique Hanssens. I'm lucky to know you all.

I am extremely grateful to the staff of the National Center for Missing and Exploited Children; to Dr. Lee Leifer; and to Mac Johnston, Barbara Benson, Tommy Pope, June Miller, Charles David Smith, McElroy Hughes, April Vinson, Tom Rouilliard, and countless others in South Carolina and elsewhere who shared their time and insight with an outsider.

This book is dedicated to the memories of Michael and Alex Smith, and to all those nameless babies who lost their lives for reasons we are only beginning to understand.

Table of Contents

Prologue

Union, South Carolina. October 25, 1994.

Alex, the little guy, always went first. Susan Smith cradled her fourteen-month-old son tenderly in her arms, arranging tiny fists, untangling the child's merrily kicking legs. The shadows of early evening were deepening in the carport of the Smith family's red-brick house as the young mother reached into the rear of her burgundy sedan and buckled Alex carefully into his baby seat. Feeling the sturdy canvas straps pull tightly against his chest, the tike heard the reassuring "click" as the fastener yielded to the will of his mother's capable hands. The ritual of the car seat was as familiar to the tot as his mother's smiling face. To Alex Smith, nattily dressed in his red-and-white-striped jumpsuit and ready to go, the back seat of his family's 1990 Mazda Protege felt like the safest place in the world.

"Mama, where are we going?"

Michael, age three, was next. Though barely past babyhood himself, Alex's older brother was a remarkably quick and observant child. That should have come as no surprise, since Susan, twenty-three, was known around her hometown as being "smart as a whip," and Michael was growing into her mirror image.

Already this evening, Michael had lit up his mother's world, Susan would say later, by declaring, "I love you so much, Mama!"—uncoached, for the very first time. Now, at the car, Michael's focus would shift to the little brother on whom he doted. He had to make sure Alex was strapped in to his seat, just right. The concern was only natural. The boys' father, David, twenty-four, recently had moved out of their home, this time apparently for good. Michael felt it was his duty to protect the baby. He was, after all, the man around the house.

Once Michael was securely in place, Susan mumbled something about going to Grandma's house. It had crossed Susan's mind to take the drive from her tiny dwelling to her mother's far plusher, split-level home in the upper-middle-class subdivision called Mt. Vernon Estates. Michael, in a blue-and-green shirt, white jogging pants, and stocking feet, was only dressed for a short excursion. He was accustomed to such trips, and would not complain. But before Susan could move the car out of idle to drive, Michael had one last, pressing concern.

"Lock the doors, Mama!"

Even in the tiny town of Union, where virtually every soul is either friend or kin, the nights can grow treacherously dark and creepy. As long as Michael Smith was in charge, no one would enter this car uninvited.

As she pulled out of the driveway, Susan's carefully glued-on expression quickly dissolved. The patient smile she kept on hand for her children contorted into something unrecognizable. The friendly mask she plastered on for the neighbors all but disappeared.

From the second the Mazda's wheels hit pavement, Susan knew her destination had radically changed.

"When I left home, I was going to ride around a little while and then go to my mom's," she later told authorities. But as the distance grew wider between the burgundy Mazda and Susan's tidy little home, the mother's darker emotions grabbed hold of the steering wheel. If Susan felt any concern for the two little boys, now falling into a trusting sleep directly behind her, she paid little mind. As the car plunged deeper into the growing darkness, Susan Smith gave in to the wave of self-pity and anger crashing inside her. The car became a vehicle for her bottomless rage.

"As I rode and rode and rode, I felt even more anxiety coming upon me about not wanting to live," she said. But what of the boys?

"I felt I couldn't be a good mom anymore, but I didn't want my children to grow up without a mom." It was a conundrum that had only one logical solution.

"I felt I had to end our lives."

Had someone watched Susan's hellish journey unfold, the sight of the young mother, on a drive with her two babies tucked in their car seats, would scarcely have raised an eyebrow. As it turned out, nobody saw. Zipping down the familiar roads of the only town she'd ever lived in, Susan was completely safe in her plan. She could carry out whatever fantasy haunted her tortured mind. And on this night, Susan had one fervent desire: to kill the pain racing through her mind.

Or eliminate the ones who caused it.

As she drove on, her captives dozing innocently, Susan passed landmarks of the major events in her limited life. There was the house in Union where Susan spent her early, pain-free childhood. And that other house, where her father went to live alone.

Until the day he put a rifle to his head, and pulled the trigger.

A few miles down a two-lane country road, and several rungs up the economic food chain, was the comfortable, split-level dwelling where her mother, after quickly remarrying, moved with Susan and her two older brothers. This was the payoff for successfully "marrying up." Here, Susan enjoyed all the riches a young girl could ask for—plentiful toys, a huge yard, and satellite TV. It also was the place where she twice attempted to take her life with a bottle-full of aspirin.

And it was the place where, Susan claimed in high school, she was sexually molested by her stepfather—a story she later recanted.

On this night, Susan knew the door would be open for her, regardless of the state she was in. But if she ever really meant to stop at her mother's place, she pressed on. Tonight, Susan did not seek the comfort of family. She preferred to wallow in her miserable self.

Passing through town, Susan could see Union High School, where she was known as something of a brain and got voted the "friendliest" girl in her senior class. It was here that she perfected the smile that would carry Susan through life, her inner self undetected. Where she learned so well to hide the demons raging within.

From the school, it's a quick spin to the huge Winn-Dixie supermarket. As a cashier in that store, Susan wooed and won the hand of the assistant store manager, David Smith, father of the two boys in the back seat. Later, it was in this store that Susan became convinced, with more than a little justification, that David had replaced his wife's affections with those of another cashier.

"I'm tired of this. I told you to stop cheating!"

Susan's angry words still seemed to reverberate from the store's aisles as she passed by. A week earlier, with Michael perched aboard a shopping cart, Alex in her arms, Susan had stormed into the Winn-Dixie to confront her estranged husband, before embarrassed co-workers, about his infidelities.

"This has got to stop!"

There was one last feature on the wild ride through Susan's pitiful life. The tour could not end properly without a vision of the one thing for which Susan would gladly have chucked everything—David, her children, Union itself.

Three-and-a-half miles from Main Street, along a gracefully curving, tree-lined road, sits an honest-to-goodness mansion. Sitting pretty on fifty privately owned acres, the sprawling, Tudor-style marvel puts to shame even the fine home of Susan's mother and stepfather. This is the estate owned by textile mogul J. Cary Findlay. A spread that's also known around these parts as "The Castle."

More importantly, at least to Susan, here lives Tom Findlay, heir to J. Cary Findlay's name and fortune. Twenty-seven, handsome, and single, Tom met Susan while she worked as secretary to his father. Young Findlay eagerly returned the sexual ardor of the youthful mother. But on October 18, Tom dumped her, explaining in a letter printed out on his office computer that he had no desire to become an instant father.

A few miles farther, another turn, and Susan would hit the spot where, just the night before, her precarious emotions got kicked into the ground. October 24, six days after Findlay said good-bye, Susan walked into Union's only bar and saw Tom sitting there, cracking jokes with friends. Susan plopped herself down three barstools away from her ex-lover. But Tom never spoke to her. The Catch got away.

*   *   *

Susan traveled ten miles out of town, down the dark, deserted reaches of a narrow, two-lane road named Highway 49. The journey was nearing an end. She had but one more turn to make.

By the time Susan veered off the pavement and steered down the path toward John D. Long Lake, Michael and Alex were fast asleep. It was approaching 9 P.M. The lake shore was deserted.

The moon, two-thirds full, cast a dull light as Susan positioned the Mazda on the cement-and-gravel boat ramp that slopes downward into the water. For a fleeting moment, she considered stepping on the accelerator, and going into the lake herself.

"I did go partway, but I stopped," she said. "I went again and stopped. I then got out of the car and stood by the car a nervous wreck."

After three hours alone in the dark with her thoughts, Susan had decided how her twisted life's journey was going to play out. And suicide was not on the program.

The Mazda was close to the water's edge when Susan abruptly popped open the electronic door locks, the ones Michael so adamantly insisted remain shut. With her sons still gripped in their car seats, Susan stepped out of the driver's seat, quickly slamming the car door behind her. From the shoreline, Susan saw the burgundy sedan roll down the boat ramp. Striking the water, the car floated off, for what seemed an eternity, along the lake's cold, still surface.

Slowly, the car filled with water. As the front end grew heavy with ballast, the Mazda rolled onto its back, and descended, upside-down, to the murky, catfish-laden bottom.

Susan Smith's life, as she knew it, was finally was over. Now, it could begin anew.

The wail pierced the darkness like a knife in the gut. It was the shriek of a woman, in agony.

Her screams sliced through the walls of a rural house sitting off Highway 49, and fell on the ears of Shirley and Rick McCloud and their son, Rick Jr., twenty-three. Opening the door, the McClouds found a young woman, wild-eyed and shaking.

"He's taken my kids in my car!" she blurted. "A black man has taken my kids and my car!"

At first, they could barely make out what the woman was saying.

As the young woman caught her breath, the family listened, spellbound. It was a horrific tale, spun by a girl they may have recognized from around town, but did not know personally.

"I was at a red light. This black man put a gun to my head and told me to drive. I asked him why he was doing this. He told me to shut up or he'd kill me."

The young woman said she drove around for miles with the gunman in the passenger seat, until he ordered her out of the car near the McCloud residence.

"Can I take my kids?" the mother told them she had pleaded.

"I don't have time to get them out of the car seats," was the man's curt reply.

By her account, the carjacker did, however, find time to promise that he wouldn't harm the children. As the man leaped into the driver's seat and sped off, Susan said, he left her standing along the highway, crying out to her lost boys.

"I love y'all!"

The harrowing 911 call, placed by Rick McCloud

Jr. at 9:15 P.M., didn't take long to fall on the ears of Union County's sheriff, Howard Wells. At forty-two, Wells was up to his eyeballs with open-container violations, drug busts, and domestic disputes. But a carjacking? And double kidnapping? In Union?

It was clear from the start that the case of the missing boys was big—far bigger than even the best little sheriff's department could handle. This case would require help from on high. State law-enforcement agents, certainly. The FBI, surely. But this case was even more monumental than that, and Union immediately sent out for the big artillery: The Media.

The carjacking story was put out in time for the local eleven o'clock newscasts, all of which dutifully reported the breaking story of two little boys kidnapped by a mysterious black man. By morning, the crime became eye-popping national, front-page news. And by October 26, sleepy Union, South Carolina, geared up for the onslaught of satellite trucks and correspondents, all of whom asked the same perplexing question: Where are they?

Over the next nine days, every flat surface in Union was plastered with artists' sketches of a black face topped by a knit cap—Susan Smith's description of the suspect. The drawings were posted alongside a growing carpet of yellow ribbons, each one a colorful prayer for the boys' safe return home.

And then there was Susan, now united with the boys' father, begging over the airwaves for someone, somewhere, whoever he was, to return her precious children.

"I can't even describe what I'm going through," the distraught-looking mother announced to the world. "I mean, my heart—it just aches so bad. I can't sleep. I can't eat. I can't do anything but think about them."

And in another, presumably heartfelt speech:

"I want to say to my babies that your mama loves you so much, and your daddy—this whole family loves you so much. And you guys have got to be strong . . . I just feel in my heart that you're OK, but you've got to take care of each other, and your mama and daddy are going to be right here waitin' on you when you get home. I love you so much."

If Susan was living a double life, Sheriff Wells was ripped in two. While the nation was captivated by the issue of city-style crime invading the rural heartland, breaking the heart of a young mother, the sheriff had more immediate worries: He knew her.

Sheriff Wells was a close friend of Susan's older brother, Scotty, thirty-two. Scotty had named Wells godfather of his two young sons. It may have seemed appropriate for a family friend to lead the investigation. Susan trusted Howard Wells.

But there was a problem. From the start, virtually from the moment Susan Smith spun her riveting tale of a gun-wielding black man pouncing at a deserted stop light, the story never added up. Even to Sheriff Wells, it just didn't make sense.

First of all, why would a desperate black man kidnap two white babies? Where did he expect to hide? And if he was running from a crime scene, as Susan suggested, why was no crime reported on the night of the carjacking? And where the heck was the car?

Authorities walked a dizzying tightrope around the young mother. Cops feared that if she knew where the children were, and detected their doubts, she might panic and harm the boys, or herself. But Susan held another, all-important card in her hand: The possibility that she was telling the truth. If law-enforcement failed to take her seriously, and the children wound up dead as a result, there would be hell to pay, and worse. The sheriff was far from the only man in Union County who would never forgive himself.

And so, two investigations were launched. On the one hand, search parties combed the region, by air and by land. Divers plumbed the murky depths of John D. Long Lake. Tips poured in—a burgundy car was spotted in North Carolina, a little boy was found in Seattle. One by one, each lead ended in disappointment.

Meanwhile, authorities were gingerly tightening the noose around the woman who had become their prime suspect.

Complicating matters even more, all over the nation and points beyond, a worried public by this time had become thoroughly caught up in Susan Smith's plight. As if in reply, each day her public entreaties grew more anguished, more detailed—more newsworthy.

"The night that this happened," Susan said on November 1, "before I left my house that night, Michael did somethin' that he's never done before. He came up to me, and he put his arms around me, and he told me, 'I love you so much, Mama.' And he—he's always told me he loved me, but never before, not without me telling him first." Then, the prayers.

"I have put all my trust and faith in the Lord, that He's taking care of 'em, and that He will bring them home to us."

But if Susan Smith was beginning to believe her own carjacking fable, she could not convince the polygraph.

Do you know where the children are? Each time the question was asked, the machine was sure: Susan was lying.

Finally, as the days passed without a ransom

demand or credible lead, the little, nagging questions kicked up the largest doubts. Such as, How does a strange man jump into a car that is known to be kept locked by a vigilant three-year-old?

Susan's charade ended on the afternoon of November 3, at a point when the citizens of Union were losing hope that the children would ever be found alive.

It was dark out when Sheriff Wells approached the microphones set up before Union's tan brick court-house—the same spot where, just days before, he had earnestly deflected rumors that Susan may be involved in the kids' disappearance.

"The vehicle, a 1990 Mazda driven by Smith, was located late Thursday afternoon in Lake John D. Long near Union," Wells began.

"Two bodies were found in the vehicle's back seat."

As the assembled crowd gasped, Wells announced that Susan Smith had been placed under arrest, and would soon be charged with two counts of first-degree murder. Then he strode away from the mike, refusing to answer a single question.

A deafening outcry tore through Union, and echoed across the nation. In a child's heartbeat, what began as a terrible tale of Stranger Danger faded into something worse. Suddenly, the biggest threat to the nation's children no longer appeared to be the unseen hand of a faceless outsider, but the familiar form of the mother next door.

"You murderer!"

Cries of rage replaced tears as Susan was ushered into the back door of the courthouse. As Union prepared to bury Michael and Alex, the collective outpouring of grief grew larger than the town could contain. A child-killer was hideous enough. But

Susan had toyed with their emotions for nine long days as she spun her web of lies. The people of Union believed in her. And she played them like saps.

Around town, yellow ribbons were swapped for blue or black. Folks talked loudly and angrily about the death penalty. And through long and sleepless nights, imaginations burned with nightmarish images of the last, horrible moments of life for Michael and Alex.

On and on, the hordes continued to descend on Union. First the media. Then came the average citizen— mothers and fathers, many toting little ones. All were drawn to the shores of John D. Long Lake, anxious to answer a single, burning question: Why?

Why would a mother kill her own children?

As a columnist for the *New York Post*, I traveled to Union to chronicle the wrenching saga of Susan Smith. Though the community was badly wounded by the ordeal, and the families involved—Susan's and David's—devastated, I was able, through interviews with numerous friends, family, and law-enforcement sources, to piece together a compelling tale of a woman who for twenty-three years walked among us, the picture of a well-adjusted neighbor, loving wife and daughter, and nurturing mother. Susan Smith. The name alone sounds so average. So *ordinary*.

That is precisely what makes this case so chilling.

Before reading on, be forewarned: The one thing this book—or anything else, for that matter—will not be able to answer with any degree of adequacy is "Why?" With this book, I do attempt, however, to answer a related question: "How?"

How did a young mother—pretty, smart, and

blessed with loving friends and a supportive family—
turn into a monster?

And how many more Susan Smiths are out there?

1

Placid Surfaces

City of Hospitality? Ha! They should call this the City of Adultery.

—Resident of Union commenting on town's nickname,
October 1994.

The weather itself is deceptive.

Deep into October, the merciless Southern sun pounds a beat along the woodsy underbelly of rural South Carolina, extending the summer to seemingly unnatural lengths. At the first clang of the school bell, long pants and dresses peel off en masse as children trot off to toss footballs in cutoffs and bare feet. From the dome-topped courthouse on Union's bucolic Main Street to the brick cottages that have housed generations of textile workers, front porches fill to capacity, awash with iced tea and talk. Neighbors wave from the parking lot of the shiny, new supermarket—

Union's one concession to progress. Down the road, the plant drones into the next of an endless series of uninterrupted shifts, each one indistinguishable from the last.

As the long, lazy morning melts into yet another featureless afternoon, the soothing sameness becomes unsettling to an outsider. It is but a short leap over the imagination's picket fence from this modern-day Mayberry into the realm of science fiction. Like a character in the movie *Groundhog Day*, one might easily become convinced he's trapped in a village where each new day is a repeat of the last. Only here, the calendar changes. Everything else appears exactly the same.

Union need not worry, though, because in these parts, outsiders are few. The town's remote geography makes sure of that. It would be easy for a motorist, driving thirty miles down Highway 176 from Spartanburg en route to Columbia, to cut right through town—maybe even stop and grab a burger at Union's roadside McDonald's—and be on his way without ever realizing he'd set foot in Union. Not that he would care. Union's lack of a movie theater, tony restaurant, or decent hotel and its dearth of well-paying jobs conspire to put off strangers. Union has always seemed to like it that way. Its secrets are safe.

When change does come, it arrives late at night. Creeping into town, like cold, disembodied fingers groping the sun-kissed landscape, autumn sneaks in through the back door. By late October, the steamy, summerlike midday heat is liable to drop ten, twenty, even thirty, degrees each time blackness overtakes the sparsely populated wilds of Union County. Traveling stealthily in the dark, the approaching season drops its calling card along the banks of John D.

Long Lake. By morning, the tranquil surface of the man-made pond casts a perfect reflection of the frost-touched pine trees. The smooth water is afire with shades of red, yellow, and purple.

The reflection is a mask.

Dip below the serene exterior. Reach beneath the calm surface. John D. Long Lake is not what you might expect. The temperature is far colder than the lake's superficial beauty might suggest. Invisible to the land dweller, catfish, that ugly staple of Southern cuisine, swim in large, hungry numbers.

Now, try to touch bottom. It escapes you. This water is unexpectedly deep, the lake bed exceptionally muddy. Just when you think you've hit the ground, a crevice digs even farther into the earth. Miss the hole, and you may never know where the lake ends.

But never mind. These secrets will remain hidden from view, for a very long time. For the town of Union, John D. Long Lake is the perfect mirror. Like Union, it takes care to conceal what lurks within.

Susan Leigh Vaughan was born as Union was in its death throes. It was 1971, and textiles, the lifeblood of Union County, its main reason for existence, were being manufactured far more cheaply through nonunion, low-wage labor in Mexico and Asia.

Rural South Carolina was in a state of economic collapse. It began in the 1960s, with the exodus of several key employers. Milliken closed two textile plants in Union County alone, throwing hundreds of workers into the wilderness.

The grand estates of the mill owners—many of them former cotton plantations that once thrived on slave labor—were going to seed. Bungalows that housed descendants of Scotch-Irish millworkers, who settled the area in the late 1800s, lay vacant and forlorn.

Young people, many of whom can trace their family trees in Union over a century, led the massive out-migration, settling in South Carolina's capital city of Columbia, in Charlotte, North Carolina, and many points farther north. In the '70s, education was in. Skilled manual labor was out. Union, it seemed, might not survive.

But the Vaughans weren't going anywhere.

Susan's mother, Linda Sue, was a hometown girl. She grew up in the community of Buffalo, adjacent to the city of Union, where a giant, redbrick mill casts its shadow over virtually every porch, church, and general store in town. It may not be much, but it was home.

"She was a beautiful girl, everybody just loved her," remembers Linda's childhood friend, Lorene Vinson.

"Like her daughter, Susan, she was real smart in school."

Academic gifts notwithstanding, Linda was still a teenager when she married Harry Ray Vaughan, a strikingly handsome millworker and volunteer fireman. Linda dropped out of high school and the couple moved into a neat, little house in the town of Union. Teen brides were nothing unusual in these parts. Even today, Union County's recreation-starved residents are known to marry early, and often.

It wasn't long before Harry and Linda Vaughan had a son, Michael. Thirteen months later, Scotty was born.

Nine years after Scotty's birth, on September 26, 1971, the Vaughans finally had the little girl they'd waited for. They named her Susan Leigh.

In the beginning, hers was a simple childhood.

Union in the early '70s was nearly oblivious to the

massive social, political, and sexual upheavals gripping minds and bodies across the nation. Cut off from the rest of creation, the community was almost entirely self-contained. It had to be. It would be another twenty years before the powers-that-be constructed the first four-lane road to ever pass through Union, Highway 176. It was another three years, in June 1994, before Union's first bar would open its doors.

The highway eventually did more to change the fabric of the close-knit region than anything in the previous two centuries. Overnight, travel time to the city of Spartanburg, and its airport, would be cut in half, to around forty-five minutes. For the first time in history, folks could catch a movie in Spartanburg on a Friday night—and still make it home in time for Letterman. In the highway's wake, progress would march on in the form of chains known everywhere but here: Pizza Hut, McDonald's, Winn-Dixie.

It is unlikely Susan Vaughan could have predicted any of this. The Union in which she learned to walk, talk, and ride a bike was virtually indistinguishable from the world of her grandmother. Aside from deer hunting and fishing, going to church remained Union's primary social focal point. And many were represented—Baptist, all brands of Protestant, even a tiny Catholic house of worship. In fact, when it was incorporated as a city two centuries earlier, Union took its name from the peaceful "union" that existed among the young village's many churches.

Later on, Union would also be dubbed the "City of Hospitality." Applying the moniker to this isolated burgh might strike the uninitiated as a little odd. "I've lived here twenty-five years," says Barbara Rippy, sixty-one, "and some people still see me as a newcomer."

Spend some time around the county, and you realize that Union's innate "hospitality" probably has little to do with the welcome extended to its infrequent visitors.

As one lifelong resident put it:

"The City of Hospitality? Ha! They should call this the City of Adultery."

As folks in Union know, boredom has a way of finding its own relief.

Its peccadilloes are masked by a convincingly wholesome facade; a snapshot of Union, population 10,000, could be used to illustrate an encyclopedia listing for the term "family values." But scratch the surface, and some of the squeaky sheen wipes off on your hand. Even the tidiest shutters and friendliest smiles can disguise trouble.

Within the picture-perfect Vaughan home, turmoil raged.

Susan was not quite seven at the time and she may not have seen it coming. Her young life was about to undergo tremendous upheaval. It was a shock from which friends and family, with the benefit of hindsight, now believe she never recovered.

Harry Vaughan, Susan's handsome father, moved out of the snug house of his wife and children and rented his own place. On December 7, 1977, Harry and Linda officially divorced.

A month later, a rare carpet of snow covered the ground as Harry Vaughan, in a fit of despair over his demolished family, lifted a rifle to his temple and pulled the trigger.

In Union, a suicide makes news, and most townsfolk learned the details of Harry Vaughan's self-inflicted death from radio reports. Wherever Susan turned, the grisly truth was visible in the pitying eyes of neighbors.

Susan cried in school the day the news broke, remembers her pal, Stacy Hartley. This would be the last time, for a very long while, that anyone can remember Susan letting her emotions show. From then on, no matter how abominable her grief, Susan learned to paint a brilliant smile over her pain.

Maybe she was born that way.

"It's typical of these people—Scotch-Irish, Protestant, ten-generations removed from those who came here to work in the textile industry," explains Mac Johnston, executive director of Union's Chamber of Commerce. "They don't show emotions much. They're very cautious people."

Even her brother, Scotty, who was fifteen when his father shot himself, had no clear idea that the event might have had a traumatic effect on his sister.

"Susan was very attached to him," Scotty says of his father.

"One would assume [the suicide] had a major effect on her. I wish we would have talked more about it."

A stoic exterior is an attribute that would always come in handy. Susan's self-possession, so common in these parts, would be used years later to help explain why, after she reported her children's disappearance, the young mother's eyes remained virtually free of tears.

Like her father, who hid his anguish until he could take it no longer, she fooled everyone.

The one childhood friend in whom Susan confided her sense of loss was Stacy Hartley, a frequent visitor to Susan's house. Locked in her room with her pal, Susan felt free to dwell on memories of her dad. Harry Vaughan, Stacy remembers, was the kind of guy who always bought candy for the children, no matter how tight money was. He always had time to spare for his little girl.

"She had an eight-by-ten picture of her father

that she kept in her bottom drawer, along with her coin collection," says Stacy.

"She would play this tape recording of him teaching her how to talk as a baby. We'd listen to the tape. We used to laugh. She was just a baby."

A short time after her ex-husband's death, Linda married a man named Beverly Russell. Bev Russell was tall and sturdy. And, in contrast to the blue-collar millworkers Linda knew from childhood, he had made a considerable living as a stockbroker and tax consultant, then opened a successful store, Bev's Appliances.

Politically active and ferociously connected, Russell was a member of the state Republican Executive Committee. Leaving no question as to how far right his political convictions tilted, Russell served on the advisory board of the Christian Coalition. Founded by the Rev. Pat Robertson, the ultra-conservative Coalition raises cash for office-seekers around the nation who, among other things, oppose abortion and favor the teaching of creationism in public school.

To Union, Beverly Russell was bona fide gentry. For Susan and her mother, he possessed the one magic ingredient the Vaughan family had never observed in quantity: Money.

After the wedding, the Vaughan children moved with their mother and stepfather into a spacious split-level home in Mt. Vernon Estates. The subdivision, carved into farmland, skirted by forest, boasts a collection of large, new homes—no two built in the same architectural style. For children, the area offers ample yard space, and hardly any traffic.

Glancing at the Russell house, though, something looks not altogether right. It takes a few moments to figure out what is wrong with this picture. Suddenly, it hits you: The property is virtually barren of trees. In fact, the whole subdivision appears oddly bald.

It's as if, in their zeal to cut a swath through nature, Mt. Vernon's builders slashed and burned every living thing in sight, making certain that a visitor's eye will be drawn to the biggest objects in the frame—the houses. The gracious assortment of mismatched structures, one larger than the next, seem to compete for the approval of envious onlookers.

The house signified a giant improvement in the Vaughan family's circumstances. Still, a few things got lost. Stacy Hartley says she never felt as warm or as welcome as she did rocking with Susan in the hammock on the lawn of her friend's little house in Union.

For Susan Leigh Vaughan, however, the house in Mt. Vernon Estates represented her first taste of what real money can buy. Her sudden good fortune, coming so close on the heels of her father's suicide, carried a lesson Susan was unlikely to forget:

Death, even of someone you love, does not mean the end. Sometimes it leads to better things.

Ask anyone what Susan was like in high school, and the first word that inevitably flips off the tongue is "nice."

"She was a real nice girl, so sweet to everybody," says former classmate April Vinson, twenty-three, whose mother-in-law, Lorene, was a classmate of Susan's mother, Linda.

"She was smart as a whip," April adds.

"She was just a terrific person," echoes another classmate, Lisa White, twenty-four.

Flipping through the yearbook for Union County High School's class of 1989, Susan Vaughan appears to be an exemplary leader. Her perky smile greets the reader on page after page.

She emerges as an energetic joiner—popular, civic-minded, scholarly. On one page, Susan, wearing eyeglasses and a conservative, calf-length skirt, accepts an academic award. In the next installment, she has tossed off the glasses and pouffed up her hair, proving she's capable of looking every bit as pretty as any gal who devotes her life to hair and makeup.

Not alluded to on any page, however, is another of Susan's preoccupations: suicide. Nor does the yearbook mention Susan's shocking allegation that the man who raised her, a pillar of local society, was molesting her.

Susan's first known suicide attempt came at age thirteen. Court documents filed by the prosecution in her murder case state that she swallowed a large amount of aspirin. Perhaps not the most lethal of drugs, but it was enough to qualify as an attempt on her life. Or, as others would suggest, a desperate cry for attention.

Though she was careful never to talk about what she was going through, word of Susan's attempts on her own life became a topic of chatter in the halls of Union High School. Some former classmates remember a period in which she disappeared for weeks. Yet in the best Deep South tradition, Susan's pals were too polite to confront their friend about her problems. They saved that topic for discussion behind Susan's back.

For a troubled girl, Susan had a way of throwing herself into each new activity as if her life depended on it. As an adolescent, she was uninterested in emulating the stereotypes beckoning the young girl coming of age in the Deep South: Texas Cheerleader.

Georgia Peach. Redneck. Belle. Good ol' Girl. Perhaps the small-town environment provided her with more down-to-earth role models. Or maybe Susan was just too brainy.

She would, however, embrace one typically Southern trait completely: Susan was the girl who aimed to please.

She was a member of the National Honor Society and joined Union High's Beta Club, whose membership was reserved to students maintaining academic averages of eighty-eight or better. She joined her school's Math and Spanish clubs, and participated in Red Cross. As a member of the Civitan Club, she worked tirelessly to make her hometown even more hospitable than it was cracked up to be.

Susan volunteered to work with the elderly, and helped raise money for Union's Special Olympics. While her talents leaned in the direction of books and good deeds rather than athletics or the arts, she did appear in one play, *Love is in the Air*. Its proceeds were donated to Children's Hospital in Columbia.

Susan fell in with a crowd of popular achievers like herself. No majorettes or football stars among them, they represented the best and brightest Union had to offer. The ones who, if only they cared to stay, would help oversee the town's eventual merger with the rest of the planet.

By most accounts, Susan was not precocious in terms of the opposite sex. Whether too shy, or simply otherwise involved, she went on what was considered a normal number of "dates," but had no lasting romances. For a brief while, her friend April Vinson remembers, Susan dated a black student. Just a few years later, interracial couples would stroll proudly along Main Street. But as recently as the late '80s, this kind of liaison still carried a strong social stigma, and kids around school freely condemned even the most casual black-white pairing.

"A lot of people said they didn't like a white girl with a black guy," says April. "More than that—some just couldn't even picture a white girl and black guy together."

Susan's daring friendship ended when the young man moved, and she emerged from the episode unscathed. But she did gain a powerful insight, one that was bound to stick. Susan learned a great deal about what it takes to push people's buttons. It was knowledge that she would draw on in the future.

In retrospect, the constant swirl of activity in which Susan centered herself appears to be a ploy. Keeping occupied, every minute of every day, was Susan's method for shoving unpleasant feelings out of her consciousness, for keeping her demons at bay. Of course, it couldn't possibly work. And as the tension grew ever greater inside her, Susan found increasingly alarming outlets for relief.

During her senior year, Susan approached the school guidance counselor, Camille Stribling.

"My stepfather is molesting me," she proclaimed.

Despite Beverly Russell's standing in the community, the counselor dutifully reported the accusation to the office of then-Sheriff William Jolly.

But then, Susan had a long talk with her mother. Abruptly, she dropped her complaint. The sheriff, with no witness and not a shred of independent evidence that anything was amiss in the Russell household, abandoned the investigation in early 1989.

What exactly happened between Susan and her stepfather, if anything, may never be known. But given Susan's proven track record as a compelling storyteller, many in Union, hearing of the molestation claim, today believe that Susan was more than capable of fabricating a tale of sexual abuse.

A year after she accused her stepfather of molesting her, in November 1989, Susan, then eighteen, swallowed another stash of aspirin. This suicide attempt, coming six months after high-school graduation, was serious enough to land her in the psychiatric ward of Spartanburg Regional Medical Center, according to court documents. She stayed in the facility for one week.

But in that spring of 1989, as Susan prepared to graduate, she exhibited not one outward clue about the drama to come. In fact, almost immediately after Susan made the sex-abuse complaint, came her crowning achievement.

Of all the honors bestowed upon seniors at Union High School, Susan won the title of "friendliest" girl in her class. This was no small distinction. In a part of the country where people place an extremely high premium on acting nice, Susan took the prize. That smile, it seemed, was going to take her places.

As Susan walked out of the doors of Union High School for the last time, nobody would have been surprised to learn that Susan Vaughan was the woman who would one day bring international fame to her hometown. What they never would have guessed is the manner in which she accomplished that feat.

2

Portrait of a Marriage

*When I heard Michael's first cry, I just started crying
  with him.*
*I had given birth to the most beautiful baby boy in
  the world.*

—From Susan Smith's album, "Baby's Milestones,"
October 1991.

Susan Vaughan didn't pay much attention to good-
looking David Smith as they passed in the halls of
Union High School. A year older than Susan, David,
with his pale blue-green eyes and slim build, was
judged "cute" by the girls in town. But that was
where the impression ended.

In contrast to the whirl of activity on which Susan

thrived, David pretty much kept to himself. The 1988 Union High yearbook carries the snapshot of the clean-cut senior. Aside from that, the book bears not a single mention of a club or extra-curricular activity in which he participated or an honor he received. In every department—smarts, social skills, class—Susan left David in the dust.

Teenage David had no time for all that. He was a working man. After high school, he went straight to his job at Union's Winn-Dixie supermarket, working his way up from bag boy to department manager before earning his high-school diploma. David's grades were nothing to crow about, and his mother tried to discourage him from spending all his spare time bagging groceries and stocking shelves. But David was relentless in pursuit of extra cash. He saw this job as the ticket to the things he wanted most. A car and a house for starters. Then, maybe, bigger ones.

When he was about seventeen, David presented his steady girl at the time with a diamond ring and asked her to marry him. Unlike so many other kids his age, David Smith had no plans to leave Union, and no interest in attending college. He would marry his girlfriend, buy a house and settle down. His future was set. Or so he thought.

Later on, this intense interest in amassing things material was one trait that would draw Susan and David together. It may not have looked that way in the halls of Union High. But the pair had quite a bit in common.

David was born in Royal Oak, Michigan, the home state of his father, Charles David Smith. A trim ex-Navy man who also answers to the name David, the elder Smith joined the peacetime military of the 1960s, only to find himself in the thick of war in Vietnam.

Later, he would advise his son, with a characteristic sly grin, "Make sure to be a conscientious objector."

In 1968, while stationed in the San Francisco Bay Area, David Smith Sr., then twenty-two, married Barbara Martin. Though she was just twenty, Barbara, a native of Spartanburg, South Carolina, was divorced and raising a son, Billy. The young family soon moved to Michigan, to be close to David Smith's family.

The Smiths' first son, Daniel, was born in 1969. David, named after his father, came along a year later, on July 27. David was two when his parents decided to pull up stakes and try life down South, and they settled in the tiny city of Union, to be near Barbara's kin. The town, circa 1972, had almost nothing to offer twentysomethings in the way of entertainment. No bar. No movies. And, at the time, a pathetic selection of retail shopping opportunities.

"But we could leave the kids' toys outside at night and they'd still be there in the morning," Smith explains. The Detroit area had grown far too dangerous, they felt, for raising youngsters.

Of course, Union County presented its own set of hazards. Barbara remembers doing the wash with her husband and younger son one Sunday at a coin laundry in the community of Buffalo, when a dog came in and bit little David Jr., who was two at the time. The parents rushed little David to the hospital for stitches. As it turned out, the dog's owner was a local minister. But when the Smiths demanded that he pay for the boy's stitches, the parsimonious preacher replied, "It's your fault. You shouldn't have been washing your clothes on Sunday."

"There's a lot of hypocrisy in Union," Barbara says now. "But there also are some very nice people."

The elder David Smith embarked on a succession

of jobs. He worked as a carpenter for a few months, then landed a job at the Wamsutta textile plant. As the fabric-making industry underwent massive retrenchment, he was laid off. Smith went to work for the city of Union, first as a mechanic, then a meter-reader. Money was in sporadic supply, but that was fairly typical among rural families in those days. Neither high-flyers nor dirt-poor, the Smiths carved out lives as regular folks.

In 1975, the Smiths had their third and last child, a daughter. They named her Rebecka.

Union's Wal-Mart discount store opened its doors in 1984. In a short while, this branch of the huge retailing giant would eat up, PacMan-like, much of the business previously enjoyed by the smaller, individually owned department stores that long had dominated local shopping. The store represented Union's entry into the modern world. It also opened new opportunities for an underemployed father. In 1984, David Smith Sr. started work as a stockman at the new store, then was promoted to customer-service representative, and, ultimately, to the ranks of management. Retailing apparently ran in the Smith men's blood.

Just as this job represented a vast improvement in the family's financial picture, tragedy came calling. The Smiths were forced to confront the fact that their elder son, Danny, was seriously ill. At eleven, he was diagnosed with Crohn's disease, a chronic, painful and debilitating condition that attacks the lower intestinal tract. He may have inherited it from Barbara, who suffered from intestinal complaints.

In just a few years, Danny Smith turned from one of the tallest in class to the shortest student in his grade.

When Danny was eighteen, his mother began

sending him to a hospital in Atlanta for periodic treatments. But the boy grew lonely, and eventually decided to seek medical care in the relatively unsophisticated hospital in Spartanburg. Barbara blames this decision for what happened next. In February 1991, Danny underwent what was becoming routine surgery to ease the most devastating effects of his affliction. But complications arose, and he developed peritonitis. Daniel Smith died on March 4, 1991, a few weeks after his twenty-second birthday.

His death came eleven days before the marriage of his brother, David, to Susan Vaughan. Danny was to be best man.

Susan and David fell in love at Winn-Dixie. Susan came to work at the store as a cashier shortly after high school. David was dairy manager at the time. Their somewhat unlikely courtship blossomed among the aisles, even while David was still engaged to his high-school sweetheart.

David may have been a boy from the beaten side of the tracks, but in the professional milieu, he was a boss. At Winn-Dixie, for the first time in his life, David was in a superior position to this girl who grew up wanting for nothing. And Susan wanted him bad.

"He kept telling me she would talk to him on the breaks, say she could make him happy," says David's mother. "She worked on him that way.

"He always had that problem," Barbara adds. "He's been raised to have good manners. He's very polite. Girls like that."

Apparently, David enjoys those qualities in a woman, too.

Susan certainly had a lot more going for her than

a pretty face and friendly ways. She was, in social and financial terms, a cut above just about any of the girls in David's league. She lived in a fine home with a wealthy stepfather. She had the kinds of things David coveted.

Before he took up with Susan, David's typical Saturday night date might have entailed a shake at Hardee's, followed by a trip to the parking lot of the high school football stadium, to hang out with the rest of the gang. Being with Susan offered exciting new possibilities.

"He would say things like, 'Over at Susan's, they have a satellite dish,'" his mother says. "'You can see this and that. It was all probably very dazzling when he was nineteen years old.'"

Just as the Russell place must have appeared, all those years ago, to the eyes of young Linda Sue Vaughan.

Rumors flew around the store about dalliances Susan was said to have engaged in with other store employees. The idle talk was of some concern to David's mother. But it did not prevent David from being flattered no end that this comely, upper-crust lady should set her sights on him.

Eventually, even his wary mom got won over.

"I would always go on her line at the Winn-Dixie," Barbara confesses. "She was so friendly. She always smiled."

If Susan used her womanly wiles to snare her man, David Smith wasn't exactly unwilling prey. After just a short period of dating, everyone who knows him agrees, David Smith fell head-over-heels in love.

Susan was pregnant when the couple said "I do" on March 15, 1991. The ceremony was held at the Bogansville United Methodist Church, a few miles outside the community of Buffalo. David wanted his brother to be near him. Just a few yards from the spot where the ceremony was held sits the small cemetery where Daniel, David's choice for best man, lay buried.

Susan's pregnancy was only two months along, so it is unlikely the wedding was arranged under the threat of a shotgun, as nosy neighbors later hypothesized. Susan wore an exquisite, form-fitting white satin gown, and carried a tremendous bouquet of pink roses. David was in a tux.

The bride was nineteen on her wedding day; David was four months shy of twenty-one. Ripe ages for a first marriage in this part of the country. Susan was so nervous during the ceremony, she placed David's ring on his right hand by mistake.

Afterward, the newlyweds, intending to save money for their own house, moved in with David's great-grandmother in Union. David, and Danny before him, had each spent time there as teens, escaping the stricter rules of their mother. But the living arrangements would create stress for new couple.

Unexpectedly, however, the first serious strain on their fledgling union occurred two months after the nuptials. This emergency came on David's side of the family.

David Smith Sr. had grown increasingly despondent over the premature death of his older son, and his depression was throwing his already shaky marriage into a critical state. One weekend, Barbara took off to stay with her family in Spartanburg. Frantic with grief and despair, the elder David Smith called his son at work and threatened to shoot himself.

It was Susan, four months pregnant, who arrived at the house to comfort her father-in-law. No stranger to dramatic gestures, Susan talked him out of hurting himself.

Shortly after this incident, David Smith Sr. left Barbara, and remarried. His new wife was named Susan, like the wife of his son.

If their difficult family histories cast a pall over the lives of David and Susan, their sadness seemed obliterated by joy upon the birth of their first son. At 5:50 P.M. on October 10, 1991, two weeks after Susan's twentieth birthday, Michael Daniel Smith came into the world.

Michael was born at Mary Black Hospital in Spartanburg, weighing in at a hardy eight pounds. He inherited his mother's bright, brown eyes and jolly disposition. In early photographs, David appears enraptured by the sight of his little boy; Susan is the picture of motherly contentment. The new parents gave Michael the middle name, Daniel, in memory of David's beloved brother. Finally, they were a family.

The day after Michael was born, David's sister Rebecka gave birth to a daughter, Kailly. Though just sixteen, Becky was already married a year to Wallace Tucker, a black man. Some believe his sister's choice of husband bothered the appearance-conscious David, but he kept any apprehensions to himself. The births of Michael and Kailly had a salving effect on the bruised families. Hard times never seemed so remote.

Susan positively glowed, and she sought an outlet to express her feelings. Using ballpoint pen, the new mother recorded her delight in her new creation in one of those mass-produced baby albums, whose cover bears the printed title, "Baby's Milestones." In neat, schoolgirl's print, she gushed over Michael in a series of warm and fuzzy personal recollections.

The diary opens:

"I've been waiting a long time to see you, precious Michael.

"It was truly the most wonderful experience. When I heard Michael's first cry, I just started crying with him. I had given birth to the most beautiful baby boy in the world.

"He was having a little trouble breathing, so I wasn't able to hold him until about 10:00 that night. It was well worth the wait.

"When he was put into my arms for the very first time, I forgot about all my pain. He really lifted my spirits and touched my heart."

The word *heart* is represented not by the letters *h-e-a-r-t*, but by a little doodle of a heart. Susan was in the habit of drawing pictures of hearts on every bit of writing in which she referred to her children. Those innocent-looking cartoonish hearts would appear again three years later, when Susan again grabbed a pen to write about her babies—this time, confessing to their murder.

With Michael's arrival, baby made four—the couple still lived with David's great-grandmother. Between the duties of motherhood and the lack of privacy, Susan grew deeply frustrated. After less than a year of marriage, she moved out of the house, taking Michael with her. Susan told David, by way of explanation, that she needed time "to think."

It's unclear who was the first to be unfaithful. In divorce papers, Susan accused David of straying. Polite and soft-spoken to the point of being passive-aggressive, David never contested anything coming out of his wife's mouth. But when Susan walked out the door that first time, David was floored.

"He was so upset," his mother remembers. "He was in such a state."

David lost his trademark reserve, and took to moping. For the ordinarily levelheaded young man, such displays of emotion were highly unusual.

Susan had stern complaints about her young husband. "She told me he treated her with mental cruelty, like I said David's father treated me," Barbara says.

She attributed this to her son's relative immaturity.

"Maybe it was just that he joked too much. He didn't take her feelings into consideration."

David grew contrite. And jealous. Once, David spotted her car at the home of another man, a pal of his. Susan claimed they were just friends. David didn't believe it.

It took a little work, but he won her back. Groveling was the ticket.

"I promise if you come back," David told Susan, "I will never, ever take you for granted again." It seemed to do the trick.

The Smiths reunited. This time, they decided they'd be happier, and the marriage would grow stronger, if they moved into a house of their own.

Number 407 Toney Road is a stunning descent from Mt. Vernon Estates. Built of brick, it is a small, square, one-story dwelling in the town of Union, built for convenience, not for comfort. It does have one pleasant feature, however: a generous yard, spacious enough for a houseful of kids to romp in. It wasn't much, but it was home.

The mortgage payments, $344 a month, put a dent in their salaries, and tight finances would be yet another source of discord in the marriage. It wasn't long after they moved in that it was David's turn to move out. He moved back into his great-grandmother's.

To coin a phrase—What's sauce for the goose is

sauce for the gander. David started dating other women. Susan, now saddled with a kid, felt herself rapidly losing control of a situation she once seemed to command. Jealousy was one emotion even Susan had difficulty fitting behind a smile. She was enraged.

Susan began storming into Winn-Dixie unannounced, looking for her husband, who had risen to the position of assistant manager. As David emerged from the back room, he was confronted by the sight of his estranged wife, her face contorted with anger.

"You better stop this, going behind my back!" Susan wailed to a sheepish David.

"I know we're separated, but I'm getting tired of all this. I'm getting tired of all this.

"Every time I come here, you're somewhere else in the store with someone. This has got to stop!"

Without another word, she turned on her heel and walked out, leaving David silent in the wake of his public humiliation.

April Vinson, Susan's friend from high school, watched these outbursts from her post in Winn-Dixie's deli department. At their height, the screaming matches exploded two to three times a week. Whether the couple lived together or apart seemed to have no effect on their frequency.

Everyone in the store knew David had affairs. But it became clear that saving his marriage became a priority.

"Finally, he did stop cheating," says April.

It didn't seem to help. Susan continued berating him over his philanderings, real or imagined.

For Michael's sake, as well as their own, Susan and David gave one more stab at reconciliation. A short time later, they found good reason to try and make it work: Susan was pregnant again.

Alexander Tyler was born in Spartanburg on

August 5, 1993. A strapping, jolly baby, Alex's parents found they had stiff competition for the baby's love: Alex was the light of his older brother's life. Just two himself, Michael enjoyed bathing the baby and helping him dress. He talked to him and wheeled little Alex around the living room in toy cars. Michael seemed happier playing with the infant than with anyone else.

Susan set out to be the perfect mother. It was an arena, like high school, for which she had extraordinary talent. The boys, sparkling clean and laughing, were always turned out in the latest kiddie fashions. They frolicked on the lawn with neighborhood playmates, and never seemed to lack for the newest and best toys. All the Union matrons clucked their approval. Susan made motherhood look effortless.

The situation was not all it seemed.

Between working full-time and raising two children, Susan was forced to drop the courses she was taking as a part-time student at the University of South Carolina's Union campus. She never kicked up a fuss, but those closest to Susan knew the shrinking of her horizons, never that wide to begin with, bothered her. No one was alarmed, though. After all, all young mothers have pressures, don't they?

David seemed aware of his wife's growing dissatisfaction. In March 1994, David presented Susan with a card for their third anniversary. It contained a sweet plea to save their precarious marriage. The printed portion of the car read:

> *Time may change a lot of things in our lives,*
> *but one thing it can never change*
> *is the way I feel about you.*

David underlined the word *never* with ink. He followed the canned sentiment with these hand-penned words:

"Hang in there, sugar-booger. You mean everything to me. God, I love you!—David."

At twenty-two, Susan Smith had two children and a dead-end job. But she had a husband who loved her, family she could turn to, and a host of friends more than willing to help ease her burden by baby-sitting. She was not alone.

3
The Catch

They had one thing in common, they were good in bed,
He said, "Faster, faster, the lights are turning red."

—From the Eagles' song, "Life in the Fast Lane,"
   played on a supermarket music system.

Alex was tiny when Susan traded her Winn-Dixie apron for a power suit and took a better-paying job at the offices of Conso Products. The huge plant, sitting virtually next door to the supermarket where David still worked, manufactures tassels and assorted cloth doodads used to finish such household items as curtains, pillows, and upholstery. An enormous sign at the Union plant proclaims Conso "The World's Largest Manufacturer of Decorative Trim."

She was just a $17,000-a-year secretary. But

Susan had hit the big time—she reported directly to the company's owner, J. Cary Findlay.

Findlay was a multimillionaire from Montgomery, Alabama, who made his fortune as a corporate raider. About six years before Susan's arrival, he bought the twenty-year-old Conso plant. Overnight, he turned it into the biggest textile concern in Union County. Employing more than 530 people, Conso was leading the depressed region toward a modest reversal of fortune.

By the mid-1980s, the county had hit rock-bottom. Findlay had the good business sense to see that there was nowhere else to go but up. Raw cloth, once the area's staple product, was still being turned out apace overseas. But fabric companies were looking to the more highly skilled American work force to produce fancy, high-end dyed and printed textiles. Union was a natural place to go.

Smelling opportunity, the town got its act together, and started working to woo new business. Union was aided by the arrival of Highway 176, which first zapped through the countryside in 1991. At long last, geography was not so great an obstacle.

Union had another selling point: Cheap labor. While South Carolina workers command higher salaries than many of their Asian and Mexican counterparts, experienced Southern millworkers can still be scooped up for something like six-dollars-and-change per hour—a fraction of the wages demanded by workers in the industrial North. That kind of paycheck goes much farther down South.

The jobs couldn't have been more welcome. In 1989, thirty-eight percent of Union County residents fell below the federal poverty line. The median value of a house was just $38,000, but even that was out of reach for so many scratching out a hand-to-mouth existence. For Union residents, making tassels was far more lucrative than flipping burgers at minimum wage. Labor for Conso would never be scarce.

To the entire region, the massive tassel-maker's success marked the beginning of a slow revival of a fragile economy. To Findlay, it meant a gold mine.

Findlay further pumped cash into Union County by buying a white elephant everyone called "The Castle"—the lavish, old Nicholson mansion that sits on fifty acres of wooded land. And why not? Conso's sales for 1994 alone were projected at some $52 million. And land here is cheap.

Lord of the manor in a way even rich Bev Russell could only dream, Findlay took up residence on the estate with his wife and son, Tom. Young Tom Findlay went to work as graphics director of his old man's company. And he moved into the guest house of his father's estate. The young heir to the family fortune soon developed a particular fondness for The Castle's hot tub, a whirlpool big enough to hold a crowd.

Ensconced in Conso's inner sanctum, Susan had a clear view of the what she'd missed for so long. Someday, she vowed, I'll make all this mine.

The marriage was crumbling. Despite David's earnest promises to be a better husband, he and Susan could not get along. Jealous recriminations became part of everyday life.

Another insurmountable problem was the couple's unhealthy finances. For a pair who enjoyed the finer things in life, David brought in only $21,700 a year on top of Susan's $17,000. Growing up, David was accustomed to lean times. But Susan had never known poverty.

What she did know was that a spunky, young woman has one sure-fire escape route from a life of drudgery. It was the method she'd seen her mother succeed at nearly fifteen years before: Marry up.

Tom Findlay was unlike any of the Union lads Susan knew. He was educated and refined. And he knew it.

As Tom entered his late twenties—social middle-age in these parts—he felt no strong urge to settle down. Tom was known to squire a selection of the local fillies to a variety of functions. He was engaged for a time to a local girl, but the courtship didn't last. Tom was in no rush. For one thing, his father was preparing to open a new plant overseas, in London. Tom had no idea how long he'd be sticking around the rural South.

But he sure did know how to have a good time. Tom achieved a degree of notoriety—and envy—for the festive parties he frequently threw in the hot tub on the grounds of his home. His friends were ushered behind the locked and guarded gates of the estate, where old man Findlay employed groundskeepers and other domestic help. Most people in Union had never encountered such a rarefied atmosphere, and Tom enjoyed giving the simple girls of Union a taste of his family's awesome wealth and power.

The parties were, by all accounts, extremely well-attended.

From her desk at Conso's front office, Susan befriended the wealthy, young man whom everyone around town started calling "The Catch." She had a history of going after the man in power. For the first time since she caught the eye of her assistant manager at Winn-Dixie, Susan was smitten.

The romance, if it could be called that, between Susan and Tom was not a matter of wide public knowledge. Most of Tom's friends who were aware of it considered the pairing more of a casual flirtation. For Tom, his dad's secretary seemed a safe choice. She was, after all, married. Commitment was not on his agenda. But Susan took the relationship seriously. Perhaps more so than Tom would have realized, had he bothered to pay attention.

When you're the richest guy in town, you develop radar for girls like Susan. Girls who look at your face and see dollar signs. Susan may not have known it, but she never really had a chance.

Tom was a regular customer at Hickory Nuts, Union's first and only bar. Actually a sports-themed restaurant and tavern, Hickory Nuts features a collection of pool tables, a wooden dance floor, and big-screen TV. When it opened its doors in June 1994, Hickory Nuts raised a few eyebrows among Union's most ardent churchgoers. But if Union wanted to continue attracting movers and shakers like the Findlays, town fathers knew, it needed to give them some place to have a good time. The bar was here to stay.

At Hickory Nuts, Tom befriended the bar manager, Lorinda Robins. Lorinda is thirty-four, blonde, good-humored—and quite married. Tom was a devoted customer and loyal pal.

In a wistful moment, Union's most eligible bachelor told Lorinda about his distaste for the gold-diggers lining up for his hand.

"I wish I could find somebody who would like me for what I am—not for my dad's money," he said.

Of course, that longing for Ms. Right did not stop Tom from taking up with Susan. Apparently, when it came to the young mother, Tom Findlay was motivated by organs other than his heart or his head.

*   *   *

It was David's roving eye that sounded the death knell for the Smiths' marriage. In the summer of 1994, David moved out of the house on Toney Road. This time, he didn't stop at his great-grandmother's. He rented his own place at the Lake View Garden Apartments complex.

Susan kicked David out after she became convinced he was having an affair with the cashier who replaced Susan when she went to work at Conso. David denied it at first. But workers at Winn-Dixie often saw their assistant manager spend his breaks smooching out back with the help. It didn't take long before word got back to Susan.

Maybe it was the Muzak, or perhaps David just had enough of his marriage, but that store had quite an effect on Union's sex life.

If Susan felt any guilt over her own extramarital relationship, those feelings were lost amid her anger over her husband's shenanigans. In the summer and early autumn, long after David moved out of their home, Susan continued her surprise visits to Winn-Dixie.

In her latest round of attack, Susan enlisted the help of her children. Carrying baby Alex in one arm, and pushing a shopping cart in which little Michael sat, Susan marched into the store to confront her cheating husband.

"This has got to stop!"

David, thoroughly chastised in the presence of his sons, customers, and colleagues, grew quiet after each episode, and returned to work.

Susan filed for divorce on September 22. She'd filed before, but this time she really seemed to mean it. On Susan's behalf, her lawyer requested custody of Michael and Alex, plus child support to the tune of $115 a week—a hefty bite out of an assistant supermarket manager's paycheck. Susan would continue living at 407 Toney Road, and take over the house payments. David could see the kids as often as he pleased, provided he gave forty-eight hours' notice. As her grounds for seeking divorce, Susan minced no words. She listed it as adultery. David's.

David took his lumps without protest. He never hired a lawyer, and contested nothing. The children would go to their mother, and he would pay what she wanted. He even agreed to foot the bill for Susan's lawyer, another $290.

While their marriage may have been a horror show, Susan and David were the ideal separated couple. Although David was required under the separation agreement to give notice before coming around, Susan never enforced the proviso. David frequently dropped by to mow the lawn at Toney Road. He played with his children nearly every day. Michael and Alex were often seen toddling on the grass outside David's apartment, playing ball with their daddy.

Michael turned three on October 10, 1994, and the Smiths celebrated the event as a family. They gave their son a party at McDonald's, a little boy's dream.

As the couple's divorce drew closer to reality, Susan's world looked brighter. She was still young and pretty. Now, she set her sights on grabbing the gold ring. Susan planned to dig her hooks into the most desirable guy in town. Like her mother, she would marry up. And spend the rest of her days as Lady of the Castle.

The bubble burst with the force of a bomb blast. On October 18, 1994, Susan suffered a slight that shattered her self-image far worse than David's infidelities. Tom wanted out. This time, there was no chance for reconciliation, no grounds for appeal.

The awful news came in a "Dear John" letter. This was not a handwritten note or a typewritten missive. Tom coolly composed his words of dismissal on his office computer, then printed them out with the push of a button. He informed Susan he was breaking up with her.

Tom listed several reasons in his letter. But Susan only saw one: Her lover was not willing to raise Michael and Alex.

How could he do this to me?! Feelings of betrayal shot through Susan like electric shocks. Tom had had his jollies, and he was moving on.

Tom's abandonment left Susan more than just emotionally devastated. She was flat broke. Her monthly income, after taxes, totaled $1,096 a month. But Susan's mortgage and car payments, day-care fees, and household bills added up to $1,286. She still had unpaid medical bills left over from Alex's birth fourteen months before.

Now, Susan watched helplessly as her escape route shut in her face.

Susan could issue a magnificent tirade from Conso's roof, if she cared to. It wouldn't do any good. Tom Findlay had no desire for a ready-made family. He was gone. And he wasn't coming back.

Six days after he dumped Susan, on the evening of October 24, Tom was sitting on a barstool at Hickory Nuts, holding court, when Susan walked in with a girlfriend. It was around 8:30 P.M., and the seats on either side of Tom were filled. So Susan plunked herself on the spot nearest her lost love, three barstools away, and stared absently into a Bud Light.

"She looked a little down," remembers Lorinda Robins. The bar manager shrugged it off. Lots of people come into Hickory Nuts to unwind after a stressful day at the office.

Tom didn't acknowledge Susan's arrival. He had come into the bar with the wife of a close friend, and the pair waited for the woman's husband to arrive. Over a draft beer, Tom joked with his companion and with Lorinda.

"He's late again!" Tom teased the woman about her tardy husband.

At one point, Tom said something to Lorinda, out loud, about the two of them running off and having an affair. They both guffawed at the suggestion.

"That was a joke!" says Lorinda. "There's nothing to it. We was all just cuttin' up, having a good time. My husband works here, too. We're all friends."

Susan wasn't in on the joke. She sat in silence, tormenting herself with the sight of her former lover. The breakup of her relationship with Tom had left Susan emotionally frayed. And here was Tom, cavorting like a school boy. Acting as if nothing at all had happened.

It was more than she could take.

Tom bought a round for everyone at the bar, Susan included. Heck, he could afford it. Susan sipped her free beer without a word of thanks. No one noticed what time Susan left. But Tom was still at the bar, laughing and drinking the night away.

As far as Susan was concerned, this man had destroyed her life. As it turned out, this night was the last time Susan would lay eyes on Tom Findlay. And he didn't say one, lousy word to her.

Tomorrow, Susan decided, things will change.

4
Without a Trace

I think it takes a very sick and emotionally unstable person to be able to take two beautiful children like that, to be able to keep them from their parents.

—Susan Smith addressing the media about her children's disappearance.

It was going to be a long night.

The 911 call came into the police dispatcher at 9:15 on the evening of Tuesday, October 25. In contrast to the ghastly emergency he reported, the man's voice was calm and respectful.

"There's a lady who came to our door. Some guy jumped into her car with her two kids in it, and he took off."

"And he's got the kids?" the operator asked.

"Yes, ma'am, and her car. She's real hysterical, and I just thought I need to call the law and get 'em down here."

When cops arrived at the house of Shirley and Rick McCloud on Highway 49, Susan Smith put on quite a show. Weepy and beside herself with worry, she sobbed her way through a rough description of the harrowing series of events of a few minutes before: The red light. The gun. The desperate black man in the ski cap. The kids.

The ordeal began after Susan got off work at Conso, and picked up Michael and Alex from their baby-sitter's house near the Smith home on Toney Road. At about 6 P.M., Susan said, she stepped out of the house and strapped Michael and Alex into their car seats. From there, the trio spent nearly three hours shopping at Wal-Mart.

Afterward, Susan said, she headed out on 49 to visit her friend, Mitchell Sinclair. Mitch, twenty-four, was a guy she'd known since high school, and he was engaged to Susan's best friend, Donna Garner. A millworker who toils the graveyard shift, Mitch shared a house with his three brothers. He was accustomed to receiving visitors in the late evening before the start of his midnight shift. But the Smith family never made it to his door.

As Susan stopped the car at the deserted red light in the community of Monarch, the black man pounced.

"Shut up, or I'll kill you."

Pistol in hand, he slid into the passenger seat. With his gun pointed menacingly at Susan's ribs, the fiend made her drive seven long miles along the dark road. In the back seat, the confused children cried.

Once they reached the entrance to John D. Long Lake, the man told Susan to pull over. Then he ordered her out of the car.

At this point, the terrifying story hit a crescendo: Standing on the road, Susan said, she begged the man, "Let me take my babies!" The carjacker said no, he was in a hurry. It takes too long to unbuckle baby seats.

The man promised the mother he wouldn't harm her kids. Then he vanished into the night.

Within days, Susan would refine her storytelling to Academy Award–winning proportions. But on this night, she had an opportunity to rehearse her delivery. Police treated her gently. Her story was gospel.

As far as anyone was concerned, a carjacker was on the loose in rural Union County with two vulnerable children in his clutches. Michael and Alex must be found immediately. There was no time to lose.

For Hugh Munn, spokesman for South Carolina's elite State Law Enforcement Division—known as SLED—it was show time.

Munn received word about the carjacking in a telephone call to his home at about three minutes before 11. It was Munn's job to spread the word to the media. Until the case was solved, he would be responsible for ensuring that television, radio, and print outlets across the country stayed interested in the story of the missing children. Munn was good at his work.

By 11:15 P.M., a mere two hours after Susan's shrieks in the night, local stations carried the story of the most fearsome crime ever to be reported in Union County. Within hours, every eye for miles would be scanning the distance, searching for a burgundy 1990 Mazda Protege with South Carolina license plate number GBK 167.

For law-enforcement types, the night was just beginning.

Cops know the importance of striking while a trail is still warm, especially in a kidnapping. Armed with Susan's description of the car and the suspect,

SLED agents and Union sheriff's deputies started combing the area.

At the very least, they fully expected to find the car right away. How far could a man drive with two scared kids?

"Think about it," one law-enforcement official told *Newsweek*. "A black man steals a car with two white babies in the back seat. He's going to hang onto it? He might as well put a billboard on it, saying, 'Shoot me, I'm the guy.' He's going to dump it in a mall parking lot or on the roadside."

The night that started so dreadfully ended on an encouraging note. A report came into Union police that a car matching the description of the missing Mazda was spotted stopping for gas in Sharon, North Carolina. It seemed likely the carjacker was heading toward the neighboring state's capital of Charlotte, some forty miles northeast of Union.

Investigators expanded their search to North Carolina, Georgia, and Tennessee. It seemed like just a matter of hours before everyone could get some sleep.

"I just feel hopeless. I can't do enough."

The lead that looked so promising didn't pan out. As the long night bled into day with no sign of the boys, Susan emerged from seclusion to meet the press.

"My children wanted me. They needed me. Now I can't help them.

"I just feel like such a failure."

Susan's eyes gazed downward during her first press conference. Wispy hair pinned into a childish ponytail, sleep-deprived eyes shielded by prescription glasses, Susan spoke into a clutch of microphones before a hushed crowd assembled outside the courthouse. She looked so young. So forlorn.

David, her estranged husband, stood at her side supportively. They were in this together. Still, as pitiful as she looked, Susan managed to come off a might defensive. She was a mother whose kids were missing. And now she had to explain to all the world how she could allow her own flesh and blood to be ripped from her grasp.

"He made me get out of the car. You know, I tried to get my children," Susan insisted to no one in particular.

"I was saying, 'There's a baby,' and 'Please let me take them.' And he said no, he didn't have time for me to take them out of the car seat."

The carjacker did, however, seem to have time galore to argue with Susan.

"And he just told me, he said, 'But I won't hurt them,'" Susan added.

The detail was a good one. It took the sting away, just a little. You'd figure any guy who would bother to make such a vow must have a conscience.

"And he just took off."

Aside from briefly recounting the carjacking, Susan used her first few minutes of fame to discuss the main subject on her mind: Susan.

"I can't even describe what I'm going through. I mean, my heart is—it just aches so bad.

"I can't sleep. I can't eat. I can't do anything but think about them."

Susan's early public utterings were a tad puzzling. By Thursday, some thirty-six hours after Michael and Alex left her sight, she appeared completely defeated.

The boys were out there, somewhere. They could be hungry or hurt. They could be dead. And there was Susan, dwelling upon her own feelings of inadequacy. Her first five sentences began with the word *I*.

This could be understandable, under the circumstances. But many a mother in earshot might wonder why a woman who'd just seen her sons stolen before her eyes would chose to talk mostly about herself.

Many a cop in earshot wondered, too.

Susan made another mistake. So soon after their disappearance, she referred to Michael and Alex in the past tense. They want*ed* me. They need*ed* me. The tots had been gone barely twenty-four hours. Too soon for Susan to be resigned to their darkest fate.

And she always looked down. The cameras never once got a direct shot of Susan's extraordinarily dry eyes.

David, however, stared directly into the cameras. He alone behaved as if the case was not yet closed.

"I plead to the guy—to the man. Me and my wife plead to him to please return our children to us safely and unharmed," David implored. "We love our children very much, and we want them returned to us, safe and sound."

David probably didn't realize it at that moment, but he proceeded to broadcast a bit of information that would prove fairly significant, from a detective's standpoint. It was a detail that could be used to call into question Susan's version of events.

Whenever the family goes out for a ride, David announced, Michael waits to hear the "thump" of the Mazda's electronic door locks. If Susan forgets to hit the switch, said David, the boy always chimes in, "Lock the doors, Mama."

How strange that on Tuesday night, for the first time, both Michael and Susan forgot the script.

As an actress, Susan definitely needed work. Fortunately for Susan, she was a fast learner. She had to be. Her primary audience was tough.

From their makeshift headquarters in the Union County courthouse, a task force of one hundred police, county sheriff's deputies, SLED and FBI agents assembled to comb the woods and highways and dive into John. D. Long Lake. In the coming days, they also would sift through every word coming out of Susan's mouth. They would study her body language. And stare deeply into those dry, downcast eyes.

She didn't know it at the time. But in this hunt, Susan was ground zero.

During the first couple of days, though, police still entertained the possibility that Susan was telling the truth. After all, Susan Smith was one of the best mothers Union County had ever seen. Everyone knew that.

As the news about Michael and Alex spread like wild-fire, it seemed as if the entire population had rallied to Susan's aide.

This included David. Though he hadn't lived with his wife for months, David affixed himself to Susan's side, the picture of the loving husband and worried father.

Leaving their individual homes, the couple hunkered down together in the house of Susan's mother and stepfather. In light of what had happened, the disagreements that led them to the brink of divorce seemed awfully petty.

Within hours, friends and strangers from across the area joined in the cause of finding the lost boys. It was as if each of the county's 30,000 residents took the crisis personally. Michael and Alex were like their own. Just as David and Susan had managed to put aside their differences, local citizens ceased their internal squabbles. The people of Union grew energized in their common goal.

"Hurry home, Michael and Alex!" Convenience store marquees, usually reserved to advertise specials on milk and cigarettes, were donated to the cause.

"We're praying for Michael and Alex's safe return," read signs on local churches.

Volunteers appeared in droves. They plastered the region with thousands of flyers bearing a recent studio photograph of the children. The leaflets beseeched anyone to report the sighting of a three-year-old boy, last seen clad in white jogging pants, blue-and-green shirt, a light blue coat, socks, and no shoes. And his fourteen-month-old brother, who wore a red-and-white-striped jumper, blue-and-red coat, tennis shoes, and socks on the night he disappeared.

Next to the boys' portrait, they hung pictures of the missing burgundy Mazda. The car should be easy to spot. Its rear bumper bore a maroon-and-white sticker for the University of South Carolina.

Yellow ribbons—a traditional call for the return of absent loved ones—covered the landscape. Folks took to wearing tiny pictures of the boys on their breasts, each one adorned with a yellow ribbon. A huge ribbon festooned the house at 407 Toney Road. Neighbors made plans for Alex and Michael's welcome-home party.

Another kind of picture also was slapped up on walls and in windows for miles around. It was the sketch of a black face. A mass-produced flyer described the suspect as being in his twenties or thirties, between five-foot-nine and six feet tall, and weighing about 175 pounds. He was last seen driving the burgundy Mazda on Highway 49, with two white boys in the back. He wore a plaid jacket and blue jeans and carried a gun. On his head was a knit cap.

His profile posted on buildings and splashed on TV, the phantom carjacker leaped into the lead as the most sought-after felon in America. Where could he hide? In Union, people studied the drawing, then looked warily around them. The face, drawn by a police artist working on information gleaned from Susan's imagination, could have belonged to almost anyone.

As the search effort mobilized, family members gathered around the couple. David's father and stepmother flew in from their home in the San Francisco Bay Area, and moved into David's apartment. David's uncle, Douglas Smith, drove down from Michigan.

David's mother, Barbara, had remarried and moved near the resort city of Myrtle Beach. Like her daughter, Rebecka—now divorced—Barbara had married a black man, Adolphus Benson. Bad blood coursed between David's divorced parents, and Barbara thought it best not to risk upsetting her son. So the Bensons got into the act near their home, plastering leaflets about Barbara's grandchildren along South Carolina's coast. They hoped the region's highly mobile population would help bring in leads.

Throughout that first day, the people of South Carolina were buoyed by optimism. It was as if, through sheer force of will, they believed they could summon the boys home.

"How can they drop off the face of the Earth?" Hugh Munn's statement, coming on the first full day of the boys' disappearance, rocketed through the airwaves from coast to coast.

Munn had succeeded in his job beyond his

wildest dreams. Finding Michael and Alex became a national priority.

Reporters flooded into Union in droves. They set up camp outside the picturesque 1913 courthouse with their satellite trucks, and lounged in portable folding chairs while chatting on cellular phones. The usually wary local matrons greeted the newcomers with coffee and doughnuts. For once, outsiders were a welcome sight in the City of Hospitality.

Correspondents converged on Union from all the big cities. They came from places where, conventional wisdom falsely suggests, little boys disappear every single day, without a trace. In truth, abductions by strangers are extremely rare.

From that first night, this story of rural kidnapping gripped the nation's collective psyche, and captured the attention of the most cynical journalists. Never before had a carjacking been reported in Union County. In fact, just two homicides were committed in the previous two years—both arising out of domestic disputes.

The consensus among the media was that the kind of random, senseless crime reported by Susan Smith just doesn't happen in Union, South Carolina.

In a way, they were right.

The carjacker never materialized during the first day of the crisis. More disturbing things did.

Authorities considered their suspect carefully. The villain, as described by Susan, was in a desperate hurry to escape from . . . something. Robbery? Rape? Murder? He was on foot, so he couldn't have traveled far. Authorities examined police calls that came in from around the area that night, expecting to link the kidnapper with another crime.

They came up empty-handed. No incident involving a culprit matching the carjacker's description had been reported. In fact, no serious crimes had occurred anywhere within running distance.

Oh well, they figured, perhaps new leads would come in.

But there was something else. Deputies took a ride to the scene of the crime. What they found stopped them in their tracks.

Susan had been certain that the traffic light at Monarch was red when the man forced his way into the car. Apart from Susan's Mazda and the thug, she said, the intersection was completely deserted.

That simply was not possible.

The highway's traffic light worked on one constant principle: It remained green indefinitely—changing to red only if a vehicle approached Highway 49 from another direction, thereby tripping a control switch. If Susan had indeed been standing at a red light, another car had to be passing through the intersection as she waited.

Authorities decided for the time being to give the woman the benefit of the doubt. Susan was hysterical. Any mother in her position could be mistaken about small details.

But other questions crept into the minds of agents and deputies, many of them mothers and fathers themselves, as they scoured the nearby Sumter National Forest in search of the car, the kidnapper, and the kids: How did he get inside the car so easily? Was there no way Susan could have run that red light? Why didn't she throw her body over the hood of the car?

*　　*　　*

At daybreak on October 26, a deafening roar filled the Union sky as helicopters buzzed the treetops in search of a wayward burgundy automobile. On the ground, tracking dogs sniffed through the forest. Local men formed search parties, and took off through the woods in four-wheel drive vehicles.

Sheriff Howard Wells greeted the sunrise with trepidation. He knew he had a tough job ahead.

Wells's first order of business was to summon the FBI. This was no time to be concerned over jurisdiction. His department needed help.

With this investigation, Wells had more at stake than two babies' lives. As a Southern politician, particularly one at the helm of a nationally watched case, the sheriff had a ticklish situation on his hands. His people were out there hunting down a black man—one that fit the rough description of potentially thousands in Union County alone.

It didn't take long for parallels to be drawn between the Smith boys' abduction and the Charles Stuart case in Boston. Five years had passed since it was resolved, but the Stuart case still figured in the national conscience as one of the larger police foulups in modern history.

Stuart was driving near a housing project with his pregnant wife, Carol, in late October 1989—nearly five years to the day before the Smith boys disappeared—when someone shot them. His wife died, but Stuart suffered only a minor wound. The distraught husband told police his vehicle had been ambushed by a strange black man. In the ensuing weeks, Boston police responded by dragging black men out of the Mission Hill housing project. Hundreds of innocent men were questioned, threatened, and detained.

By the time Stuart's brother told police that

Charles Stuart had killed his wife, a black man had been charged in the murder. It was too late to make amends. The police department's overzealousness had raised racial tensions in Boston nearly to the flashpoint. Stuart later committed suicide.

The lesson of Charles Stuart was not lost on the cops in rural South Carolina. As long as Wells was in charge, there would be no repeat of the Stuart fiasco in Union.

But the inevitable comparisons with the Stuart case brought to mind another disturbing issue: In that crime, a man everyone perceived as a victim turned out to be a cold-blooded killer. The true assassin was a person no one in his right mind would have suspected in a hundred years.

Wells knew the score. To carry out his duties completely, the sheriff needed to gather all the resources at his disposal. Not only would he seek aid from afar, Howard Wells had to reach deep inside himself for strength. Because the most wrenching task in the entire investigation fell to the sheriff.

Wells was to be Susan's main interviewer. He was the man who would personally "handle" the aggrieved mother, holding her hand tenderly while pumping her hard for clues. To perform this job, the sheriff had to draw on all the training and experience he'd amassed in two decades spent in law-enforcement. Susan Smith was more than just any mother. She was his neighbor, and his friend.

She was also a suspect. Wells could not allow his feelings for Susan get in the way.

In this battle of wits, Sheriff Wells was Susan's perfect foil. Like his subject, he knew well how to conceal his thoughts behind a congenial poker face. The two had a lot in common that way.

Howard Wells is man of few, carefully chosen

words. Tall and reed-lean with a neatly trimmed mustache, Wells cuts a figure of the consummate professional lawman. He is the antithesis of every clichéd Hollywood portrayal of a gun-loving redneck Southern sheriff.

Born in Union, Wells began his career as a city police officer in 1975, when he was twenty-three, and was appointed deputy sheriff a year later. In 1980, Wells took a job as a wildlife officer with the South Carolina Department of Wildlife and Marine Resources. In a region rich with deer hunters and their many guns, being a successful game warden requires a cool head and firm hand. Wells kept the job for twelve years.

In 1992, he ran as the Democratic candidate for Union County sheriff, after the incumbent chose not to seek a new term. Two months before the election, Wells's mother was diagnosed with terminal cancer. Rushing to her side, Wells all but abandoned the hard-fought campaign. Even so, he squeaked to victory. With about 8,000 votes cast, Howard Wells was elected sheriff of Union County by a margin of nineteen votes.

The county got its money's worth. During the summer of 1994, after a year-and-a-half in office, Wells was invited to attend the FBI training academy in Quantico, Virginia. The elite finishing school for serious law-enforcement types was the backdrop for the movie *Silence of the Lambs*. In Quantico, Wells honed his investigative techniques. And he learned invaluable lessons about the criminal mind.

One lesson in particular would come in useful during the most difficult autumn of Wells's career: You can't pick the bad guy by the way she looks.

By extraordinary coincidence, a month before the Smith brothers' disappearance, the U.S. Department of Justice issued a police manual for dealing with kidnappings. Hugh Munn from SLED had helped write it. The manual's chief recommendation boils down to this: Always suspect the family.

The reason is clear. Despite the propaganda disseminated by firms that make a profit from services like fingerprinting children, abductions by strangers are rare. Two hundred to three hundred a year, according to a recent estimate cited by the National Center for Missing and Exploited Children. Most of the thousands of children who disappear each year are taken by someone who knows them. Often, that's the last person you would expect.

To quote the manual: "Understanding the highly emotional nature of a missing child case is a vital part of being able to assess the situation accurately."

Wells was the kind of lawman who liked to go by the book.

From the start, the snatching of Alex and Michael was handled with what's known by cops as a "parallel" or "dual" investigation. Two investigations, if you will, for the price of one. Finding the children—alive—was absolutely the top priority. At the same time, police surreptitiously probed the parents.

"The idea is to eliminate them very quickly, or implicate them," explains Ruben D. Rodriguez, senior analyst for the National Center for Missing and Exploited Children.

At this point, neither Susan nor David—or anyone else in the world, for that matter—had been ruled out as suspects. As searchers beat the bushes for Michael and Alex, Wells would get busy eliminating potential kidnappers, one by one. But they must never know.

It was with all the caution that came naturally to the sheriff, sprinkled with the skills he's picked up along the way, that Howard Wells approached Susan Smith in her first interview.

It would be a tough one. Because during that first day of investigation, Susan already had been caught in a lie.

5

White Lies

Any number of factors can precipitate an abduction including a separation, a contested visitation schedule, domestic violence, differences in child-rearing strategies, and/or conflicts over support payments. . . . The parent will often convince him-herself that all hope of correcting a perceived problem has been exhausted.

—From chapter on family abduction in the Justice Department manual *Missing and Abducted Children: A Law Enforcement Guide to Case Investigation and Program Management.*

"Susan, where did you *really* go last night?"

During her first interview with the sheriff, Susan was on her own. David, her parents, friends who might bolster her emotionally, were barred from the room.

Susan was taken to an armory, to escape the

reporters who followed her every footstep. Her old family friend, Sheriff Wells, handled the questioning, along with Robert Stewart, the chief of SLED.

The session started on a friendly note. Susan was the only known witness to her sons' kidnapping and investigators said they needed her help. Patiently, they prodded Susan, cajoling her to scan her memory for any detail, no matter how insignificant. Anything that could help them find Michael and Alex.

Over and over, Susan repeated her tale of the carjacking. She went through the contents of her conversations with the criminal. She described what he was wearing. How he moved. She explained the exact manner in which the carjacker slipped from the passenger seat to the driver's side of Susan's car. As far as details of the fugitive's appearance were concerned, Susan had a good excuse for being sketchy: The carjacker had warned Susan not to look at him. With a gun in her ribs and her babies in the back seat, Susan obeyed.

"Why did he take the car?"

"I don't know. He didn't say."

Susan elaborated little on her original account. Always, the questioners pulled for more.

Their goal was to make Susan expand on her story. Like everything else in this probe, there were two reasons for that. First, authorities tried to determine if Susan had somehow forgotten to divulge some minor clue that might be the key to finding the boys.

Second, the more information Susan put forward, the larger and longer the story she had to remember. If she was telling the truth, no problem. If not, investigators knew it was just a matter of time before she got her stories confused and tripped herself up.

"Why wouldn't he give you the children? What was the hurry?"

"I don't know. We had very little conversation."

Susan wasn't bad at this. She knew instinctively to limit her storytelling. At difficult junctures, she'd say, "I don't know," rather than go off on some make-believe tangent. Investigators may not have been entirely aware of her background, but Susan had vast experience in living a lie. Since she was a small child, she knew how to fool people by playing it close to the vest. She was a formidable subject. But she hadn't thought of everything.

It didn't take long for the guys to get to the point.

"Susan, we went to Wal-Mart," Wells searched Susan's face for a reaction. "Nobody saw you there last night.

"Where did you *really* go last night?"

She couldn't have seen this coming. Her friends had put her on the spot.

The night before, Susan reported that she had spent three hours with her sons shopping in Union's huge Wal-Mart discount store before taking her family on that fateful drive down Highway 49. Perhaps Susan never expected anyone to check. But investigators promptly went to the store and interviewed employees who were on duty Tuesday night. Most of them knew Susan, some of them quite well. She was a regular customer, as well as a neighbor to them all. When Susan shopped, employees always traded pleasantries with the friendly mother and her adorable sons.

It just wasn't possible that Susan could have skulked around Wal-Mart without being noticed. Especially not for three hours. And no one saw Susan in Wal-Mart on the night of October 25.

Why make up a story like that?

Susan knew she was caught, and she 'fessed up to her fib. But nothing more.

"I drove around the county for three hours," Susan told them. She said she just wanted to spend some time alone in the car with her thoughts.

Susan explained that she feared police might find all that aimless driving suspicious. She said she told them the first thing she could think of to account for her whereabouts. No big deal, right?

She was right about one thing. The little white lie was suspicious. What was she hiding?

Investigators entertained the theory that Susan had tucked the children away with a friend or relative, probably to hide them from David. This was a common occurrence in cases in which a kidnapped child's parents are separated or divorced. Parents use their own kids as pawns in their adult battles. In some instances, a parent is simply trying to protect the children from an unfit or abusive spouse. Even so, experts in the field believe a life on the run can be even more physically and emotionally damaging to young people than an unhappy home life. That's why family courts were set up to decide issues of custody.

But if Wells and Stewart believed they were dealing with a tug-of-war in which Michael and Alex were the rope, there was one thing about the scenario that didn't add up: David had never asked for custody of his sons.

Considering all the problems during their marriage, the Smiths' pending divorce was nothing if not amicable. David saw his boys nearly every day. He even cut the grass at his former home on Toney Road. Susan seemed pleased with the arrangement. She had no apparent reason to hide her children. But the probe was far from over.

David certainly had not been ruled out as a suspect. Perhaps he had the boys. It seemed unlikely, though. If David was unhappy with the visitation arrangement or if he wanted to raise his children alone, wouldn't he have said something by now?

It was of course still quite possible that Susan and her sons fell victim to a carjacker. That was too dangerous to ignore. Authorities would never forget a child-snatching case in Alabama. So certain were they that the abduction was "internal"—that is, perpetrated by a family member—they never conducted much of a search.

Eventually the child was found in California, murdered. The cops had been wrong.

With this in mind, detectives focused on finding the boys. They had to be *somewhere*. Each person in the room tried to banish from his mind any thoughts of the one fate no one wanted to consider: Michael and Alex could already be dead.

The image of their merry little faces kept investigators on track. Finding Michael and Alex alive was the only thing that really mattered. Locating the person who snatched the boys was important at this point primarily because the kidnapper could lead cops to the children. The law could deal with the villain later.

But before Susan was excused for the day, her friendly interrogators had another tiny, little question they needed her to clear up. No big deal, they insisted, we believe you. Just doing our job.

"Where were you *really* heading on Highway 49?"

Susan had said she was on her way to visit her friend Mitch Sinclair on Tuesday night. She probably didn't think anyone would check. But investigators went out Mitch's house.

Mitch told them he wasn't home that night. He hadn't been expecting company.

The search for Michael and Alex inevitably focused at John D. Long Lake. The man-made fishing hole, named after a South Carolina state senator, is a popular recreation spot in Union County. Now, the lake had gained a different sort of fame. It was near this lake, Susan said, that the carjacker relieved her of the Mazda and its youthful inhabitants. It seemed a likely spot for a man on the run to ditch a car quickly.

As they penetrated the lake's cool, reflective surface, the divers prayed. Please God, let us find the car. Just don't let the boys be inside.

Nine of the best divers in South Carolina submerged into the murky water fitted with all the fanciest equipment—underwater goggles and a sonar device designed to detect objects at the lake's bottom. They would need every advantage to tackle this assignment. The men included Sergeant Francis Mitchum, with seventeen years experience diving for the state, and Steve Marr. The father of a small child, Marr volunteered to participate in the search.

As small as the lake appears, looks can be highly deceptive. From top to bottom and side to side, John D. Long Lake comprises thousands of cubic feet. It contains countless crannies capable of hiding a car. At some points, the bottom plunges to a depth of eighteen feet. Where do you even begin to look?

From the shoreline, searchers estimated the weight, volume, and possible speed of the Mazda. Then they calculated how far a nearly two-ton automobile was likely to travel before its engine gave out and the car got mired in mud. There also was the chance that the

Mazda could float. Were its windows open or closed? What about the doors? Each potential factor required a new estimate. It was rough science, but it was the best available.

Another crucial matter was known only to the person who drove the car: The exact point at which the Mazda might have entered the water. Did the carjacker follow the lake's gravel-and-cement boat ramp? Perhaps he pushed it into the water from some point on the grass.

Donning flippers and wet suits, the divers entered the sixty-eight-degree water and carefully scanned the lake's shallow perimeter. The going was slow. This lake was even darker and muddier than anyone realized, and searchers had to feel their way along. Gradually, the divers ventured into deeper water, eventually going out a distance of thirty feet. It didn't seem possible a car could travel even that far.

They reemerged empty-handed.

On Thursday, October 27, more than twenty-four hours had passed without a clue. A sense of dread descended heavily on all 10,000 residents of the city of Union.

Whoever has the boys, the people hoped, please make sure he keeps them warm. As the calendar drew closer to Halloween, forecasters predicted the region's balmy daytime temperatures would drop below freezing after nightfall during the coming days.

The people of Union no longer felt safe. The carjacker had violated them all. With this kidnapping, the community lost far more than two lovable children. Michael and Alex could turn up tomorrow. But Union had been robbed permanently of one thing its citizens always took for granted: peace of mind.

"I won't let her play outside anymore," a young mother commented to local reporters about her toddler girl. "She hates being cooped up, but I can't help it. You don't know who's out there."

Union was the kind of place where even small children played outside independently of adults. People drove carefully. Neighbors always looked out for each other's kids. These days, mothers hovered over their babies as never before. And bedtime stories began and ended with the warning, "Don't talk to strangers."

The children grew as fearful as their parents. They clung to their mothers' sides and eyed outsiders warily. Where students once walked home from school unescorted, they now hopped the bus. The sidewalks stood empty.

It just didn't feel right. Susan's cousin Dennis Gregory, who lives in Columbia, South Carolina, called the carjacking "a crazy thing."

"That kind of thing doesn't happen here. People sleep with their doors open."

Doors, in fact, had remained unlocked so long in Union, folks had to make sure their dead bolts still operated before turning the handle. And turn them they did. It seemed things would never be the same.

The searches all came to naught. Nothing seemed to work. Even the tremendous spirit that propelled the populace into action was not as helpful as everyone hoped. As news of the Smith boys' abduction spread coast-to-coast, thousands of tips flooded the circuits of overworked police operators and threatened to jam fax machines. Each lead sounded encouraging at first blush—the car was spotted at such-and-such a location, a little boy matching Michael's description was abandoned in a mall.

Everyone, everywhere, was on the lookout for those toddlers.

"It got so that every time I saw a maroon car, I thought, 'Maybe that's the one,' says Tommy Pope, the prosecutor for Union County. Pope had professional reasons to keep a close eye on developments in the case. But he also had a son. Like everyone else in the country, he took the case personally.

On the second day of the hunt, an exciting prospect finally emerged. A lead, more promising than any before, jumped out from the stack of duds that were being amassed faster than detectives could sort through them. Once again, all eyes looked to the north.

A convenience store had been robbed in Salisbury, North Carolina, about 100 miles north of Union. The suspect reportedly took off in a burgundy car. Shortly after that, a hunter reported hearing a child crying for his mommy in the nearby Uwharrie National Forest.

Pay dirt. The robbery's close proximity to the report of a lost child sounded too good to be true. The cries alone were wonderful news. That could mean at least one of the children was still alive.

Helicopters were dispatched into the forest with haste. Each was equipped with a heat-seeking device capable of pinpointing a person in the dense underbrush. For fourteen hours, the forest was searched, by air and by foot.

The searchers turned out to be right about just one thing. The lead was in fact too good to be true.

Sheriff Wells is no showboat. Tight-lipped by nature as well as professional necessity, he's not the type of man who routinely calls attention to himself. But as

the second full day of the search for Michael and
Alex drew to a close without a sign of the children, it
was time for Wells to address the nation.

In the case of a kidnapping, appearing before the
media is a by-the-book investigatory technique. Taking
a page from the Justice Department-issued manual,
dryly titled *Missing and Abducted Children: A Law
Enforcement Guide to Case Investigation and Program
Management*:

> *Law enforcement officers know that a signifi-
> cant number of cases have been resolved
> through prompt and effective use of the media.
> Nowhere is this success more evident than in
> cases of missing and abducted children.*

Wells is nothing if not thorough. But he had a
slim line to toe. Part of his mission was to rally the
public to the cause of rescuing the children from a
fleeing black carjacker. At the same time, Wells harbored serious doubts the man even existed.

That duality shined through to the observant
television-watcher on the night of October 27, as Sheriff
Wells appeared, via satellite from South Carolina, as
guest of honor on CNN's *Larry King Live* program.

The host kicked off the show on an entirely cred-
ulous note.

Larry King: Good evening. If you drive a car, listen up. You don't want to be the victim of a carjacking. Take it from Susan Smith. Her worst nightmare
began forty-eight hours ago. And she's living it right
now.

Susan Smith (on tape): I can't even describe what I'm going through. I mean, my heart is—it just aches too bad. I can't sleep. I can't eat. I can't do anything but think about them.

With that, it was Wells's chance to speak live to the millions of homes reached by Cable News Network. He came on camera to appeal for help. At the same time, the sheriff made little attempt to mask his mystification over the more baffling aspects of an unusual case.

Wells started with a brief description of the manner in which FBI agents and police were collecting tips. Then, just as Susan had found it necessary to tell the world, somewhat defensively, how she let her children get away from her, Wells launched into an explanation of why his troops had come up with nothing after two days.

Wells: The case is very slow to unfold because we don't have a crime scene. There was nothing left behind. We can't even ascertain if the suspect was even a Union County resident or not. We're not missing anyone. We had no crimes that he would have to be fleeing from. We're at a loss right now to determine why he did it, unless it was the car he was after.

King: . . . What has Mrs. Smith told you about why this fellow took the kids?

Wells: The suspect didn't tell Ms. Smith anything, as far as reasoning as to [why] he was taking the car. They didn't have a discussion. He ordered her to be quiet, or he would harm her. He was armed with a handgun while he was in the car. They rode a short distance and he ordered her out. He did not ever mention money. He never harmed her in any way. He let her out near a home where the lights were on, knowing she could get attention.

We can't understand why, when she asked for her children, he said no, that he didn't have time. But he promised he would not hurt them.

Which led to another thing authorities had trouble explaining: Where is the car?

King: You've got good—you know what the car is. You know the license number. You've got this massive surveillance and hunt out. Can't find the car?

Wells: No sir, the car hasn't turned up. That's what's baffled us.

Usually, a car that is hot from a theft will turn up abandoned on the highway, or in some secluded area of property or woods, or in some parking lot at a shopping center. We were hoping for the latter, that if the car had been abandoned in a convenience store or shopping center, the kids may still be with the car. We haven't had sightings of the kids by themselves, the car by itself, or the suspect. So, we are assuming right now that the three are still together.

The carjacking report was suspicious, all right, and Wells did his best to tell the truth without exposing every last card in his hand. Still, it was a close call.

Forty-eight hours after Michael and Alex were last seen, Sheriff Wells may have fallen into a small contradiction contained in the Justice Department's bible for dealing with abducted youngsters.

"Very little information is so critical that a case would be jeopardized if it got out," reads a passage from the "Crisis Media Relations" chapter of the missing-kids manual.

In another breath, the same chapter warns about the danger of a media "crisis" forming in a kidnapping case.

A dictionary generally defines a crisis as ". . . a turning point or an emergency." That is exactly what happens when law enforcement agencies yield management of an investigation to the media simply by failing to recognize that incorrect—and potentially damaging—perceptions are forming.

The manual's prediction was wrong on one small point: The crisis looming on the horizon would not be sparked by "incorrect" public perceptions already forming in the Smith case. The sheriff faced much bigger problems as people formed "correct" perceptions about what really went down in this double abduction.

And this case was about to hit a turning point.

6

A Case of Race

If you're looking for a good Christian community, a quiet community that hasn't progressed in many years, this is a good one.

—Union County Sheriff Howard Wells, discussing Union's racial harmony.

Union on a Saturday night can be a boring place. The only bar in town closes at the stroke of midnight. Convenience store workers slap locks on beer coolers the instant the big hand hits the number twelve. Blue laws are still very much a way of life in the Bible Belt. When the clock says it's Sunday, the government has decreed, it's time to stop drinking and start praying.

You never know when you'll need it.

On a warm Saturday night in mid-autumn, a knot of white teenagers gathers around the Li'l Cricket convenience store on Main Street, chugging the dregs of a pre-Sabbath beer. They are two boys and two girls, hands in their pockets, out on the town with nothing to do.

The kids soon run out of people to call on the pay phone. The beer is about gone. They've got nothing to say. When all of a sudden, entertainment walks by in the form a black man clad in workman's coveralls, drunker even than they.

Crash. The beer bottle bursts. Excited expressions replace the teens' blank stares.

"Who do you think you're lookin' at?" a boy calls out menacingly.

"Cracker!" the black man yells gleefully.

"Nigger!"

"Hah!"

The white boys start after the black man, but he is already too far away to catch. Losing interest, the boys turn back to the girls. Plenty of time later for a senseless fight.

How are relations between the races in Union? On the face of it, pretty similar to relations between the sexes. It all depends on whom you ask.

The sly looks and double-takes were unnerving. Walking down Main Street, stopping in the car at a red light, a man could almost feel the eyes boring into the back of his head. Or so it seemed.

Suspicious glances. Covert whispers. Unabashed glares. Did they really exist? Or were the men who perceived these reactions just being oversensitive? In truth, the staring mattered little. People could do far worse. The situation could grow truly ugly. From his barbershop in downtown Union, fifty-nine-year-old Marty Keenan was one man who braced for what he expected would be a massive police roundup of

Union County's black men. Things like that had happened before.

Police had a serious job on their hands. A black carjacker was reported on the loose somewhere in the countryside. And in late October 1994, everyone in Union, black and white, accepted that the criminal must be found. A man who would steal a car containing small children was a threat to everyone. Besides, every citizen in Union wanted badly to see the babies home safely. Concern for the safety of Michael and Alex did not follow racial lines. The boys must be found, and quickly. All the people of Union, regardless of color, felt diminished by this heinous crime.

Just don't make us all suffer, the black community prayed.

It was so that Sheriff Wells faced yet another in a continually expanding series of investigatory dilemmas. His team had to conduct a convincing hunt for a black suspect. But it also was incumbent upon the sheriff to consider the welfare of his black constituents—not to mention the future of a county of 30,200 residents, twenty-nine percent of whom were black. A police screw-up might have repercussions that could do Union irreparable harm. What's more, the entire nation was watching Howard Wells's every move.

With all this in mind, deputies stopped and questioned a number of men who matched the vague description of the carjacker provided by Susan Smith: A man in his twenties or thirties—possibly his forties. He was five-foot-nine to six feet in height. The man they sought weighed around 175 pounds. His skin was extremely dark. And he owned a knit cap.

Lamont Cheek was only seventeen, but he was one of thousands in the local area who could fit the carjacker's description. Cheek was walking home during the first week of the boys' disappearance, he told reporters, when police stopped him and asked questions in connection with the carjacking.

Cheek talked to cops briefly, then went on his way. He had no complaints about the way he was treated by authorities. He was not hauled into the station house. There was no mention of a polygraph. But he was put on the defensive, all the same. What worried Cheek most was not the police, but all those other people who had trained their eyes to scan the streets and highways and front porches of Union, searching for a black kidnapper.

"They slowed down and looked at you," Cheek told the *Boston Globe*. "It was like all the white people were wondering if you were the guy."

Cheek said he and some friends began pulling down copies of the black suspect's sketch from walls and electrical poles around Union. It was a random, visceral response to what felt to Cheek and friends like unjust victimization. They had no cohesive plan to tear up every leaflet in town. Not that it mattered. A generic black face was seared in the mind of every person for miles. It could belong to almost anyone.

The case of Charles Stuart of Boston, the white man who shot his pregnant wife in 1989 and blamed the murder on a black gunman, was not lost on Union's black residents. They remembered vividly how police rounded up and detained hundreds of men for interrogation. To Boston cops, it seemed, these housing-project dwellers all looked alike. And that took place up North.

Fear ran high that small-town South Carolina would be even more prone to engage in the mass persecution of blacks. People who, in terms of power and economics, were Union's poorest citizens. But the town had never been a hotbed of racial politics, and black residents waited in silence. No marches of protest were planned for the area. The young men just wanted to be left alone.

For the most part, they got their wish. Only a handful of men were questioned in connection with the abduction. None was arrested.

Perhaps the restraint stemmed from authorities' doubts about Susan Smith's story. More likely, those doubts were combined with cops' heightened awareness of the volatile political climate that pervades all matters of crime and race. The videotaped image of Rodney King, a black motorist, being beaten by Los Angeles police was permanently seared into the national consciousness. So, too, were pictures of the riots that resulted from the officers' initial acquittal on the most serious charges brought in the beating. For days, black-owned stores were looted and burned. Reginald Denny, a white trucker, was beaten to a pulp by a black mob as TV cameras broadcast each blow.

At the same time, the disproportionate incidence of black-perpetrated crime remained a national reality. Speaking in an unguarded moment, the Rev. Jesse Jackson drew vast nods of recognition when he delivered his now-famous anecdote illustrating his frustration with the high rate of black crime. The black leader confessed that every time he hears footsteps while walking along a dark city street, he feels relieved to turn around and find that the person behind him is white.

And so, when Susan Smith gave her mental sketch of a carjacker's face, she had good reason to think she would be believed. In Susan's mind, it was easy to conceive of a forest filled with black faces, each belonging to a man ready to pounce at a lonely intersection.

In reality, the most dangerous place for Union's women and children is in the home.

By autumn 1994, Union County had rung up sixty-two incidents of domestic violence for the year. Murder is also a family affair. Union's last two homicides took place within families. One was committed by a woman later acquitted of killing her abusive husband in self-defense. The other was a man who killed his wife in a religious rage. Both cases involved white couples.

Brawling and boozing are the two surefire methods for a Union resident to land behind bars. During the first ten months of 1994, the county tallied 101 cases of simple assault. Violations of open-container ordinances totaled sixty-nine. The number of drug busts, on the other hand, came to four. Union does not sort its crime statistics according to the perpetrator's race.

As the sheriff was well aware, crimes by strangers in these parts are not just unusual. They are almost nonexistent. But Susan was playing to a wider audience. And she knew this crowd well.

Union's blacks and whites have a common—if uncomfortable—history. Like their white neighbors, many black citizens can trace their families back to the town more than a century. Surnames heard frequently in Union County, such as Jeter, are shared by people of both races. These are the descendants of master and slave.

More than 100 years after the abolition of slavery, there exists a chilling landmark to Union's scarred record of race relations. At a point along two-lane Highway 215 sits a clutch of three trees growing in a triangular pattern. According to local lore, every small Southern town has its infamous trees. Union is no exception.

"When I first moved to Union, people told me that was where they hanged black men if they tried to date a white woman," says David Smith's mother, Barbara Benson. "That was 1972. I got the impression it wasn't a whole long time since those trees were last used."

The Union in which Susan grew up was just a generation removed from enforced racial segregation. Her parents attended all-white schools. Many people over thirty continued to mix with black folks uneasily. Even in her own, integrated high school, Susan faced sharp criticism when she briefly dated a black student. Old attitudes die hard.

Interracial dating was slowly coming into vogue in 1990s Union, particularly among white women and black men. Susan's own sister-in-law, Rebecka, had married a black man and had a daughter by him. Rebecka's divorce resulted not from racial differences, but from her husband's infidelities. Susan's mother-in-law, Barbara Benson, also crossed the color line in her third marriage. No longer was that sort of relationship considered grounds for a lynching. But that doesn't mean everyone was happy with the modern state of affairs.

"I've certainly seen mixed couples around here, but with the older crowd, it's probably still taboo," explains Mac Johnston, executive director of Union's Chamber of Commerce.

Union entered the '90s sharply divided on the race question. White women held hands openly with their black beaus. Meanwhile, on a pole atop the local pawn shop, as well as on a scattering of houses and car antennas, Confederate flags continued to fly. The flag, to some a visual symbol as emotionally jarring as the Nazi swastika, is one relic of the past that quite a few South Carolinians stubbornly insist on preserving.

To old-timers, such as barbershop owner Marty Keenan, the flag is a constant reminder of the days immediately before and after integration, when blacks and whites brushed up against each other at great peril. It was a time when people of both races were beginning to compete for the same jobs and decent housing. For the first time, fraternizing with whites was acceptable. That is, in some circles.

Keenan is one of several blacks of his generation who described a 1952 incident in which a black man was said to have been imprisoned for years, literally because he "brushed up" against a white woman.

"He was coming through a doorway, arms full of packages when he brushed up against her," says McElroy Hughes, president of the Union chapter of the National Association for the Advancement of Colored People. "If you were black, you were not allowed to make contact with a white woman."

Tales such as this are difficult to verify, but impossible to ignore. However the 1952 incident played out, it is easy to believe that a black man in those days could have been imprisoned on trumped-up charges stemming from a perceived racial slight. A better test of Union's present-day racial tolerance is to compare how similar events are handled today.

For that, you don't have to look all the way back to the '50s. Black men were used as scapegoats for crime as recently as 1993. Just a year before the Smith boys' abduction, Hughes remembers, a white woman reported that she had been mugged and robbed of her cash by a black man. The story circulating in the black community was that the woman had gambled away the grocery money on a video poker machine and had made up the story to appease her angry husband.

A major difference can't be ignored between the

legend of racial injustice, circa 1952, and its modern
equivalent. The black men who were in each case
accused of wrongdoing were dealt with in vastly different ways. In the 1990s, blacks simply are not thrown
into jail for no reason. In some ways, little Union had
made lightning progress in the last forty years.

Still, as stories such as these pass from one generation of Union's blacks to the next, their focus has
tended to shift. Through years of retelling, the anecdotes have transformed from descriptions of fact into
cautionary tales. Blacks take them as a warning: Be
careful who you mess with.

In their own way, white people growing up in the
South face their own kind of racial prejudice. It is all
too common for outsiders to brand the entire
region's white population as racist. Perhaps it stems
from guilt over the South's long history of slavery
and segregation, or maybe folks have grown sensitive
to the criticism, but many Southern officials have
been forced to confront the issue of race in ways
Northerners, overconfident in their record, may have
ignored.

In Union, that meant authorities used extra care
to treat all its citizens as individuals. It shouldn't be
that difficult. This was the kind of place where everyone knew everyone else.

In the autumn of 1994, most of Union's residents
talked like Barbara Rippy, the white owner of
Smith's Drugstore: "This is the kind of community
that sticks together in a crisis, black and white,
where everyone helps someone in hard times."

"We get along beautifully here," echoed James
Hardy, a fifty-six-year-old retired plumber, who is
black. "A lot of black men are going with white

women. We don't have any problems," Hardy added enthusiastically. "We also don't have any problems with police. If you do something, then you get arrested."

An underpinning of anxiety belied much of this Union-boosting, as the town was scrutinized under the national microscope. So many of Union's blacks were revealed to be living in crushing poverty. The high-school dropout rate for black students was exorbitant, and illiteracy ran high.

Union never did take well to outside agitators from up North—people who would threaten to rock the town's equilibrium to benefit a cause.

"The community at large has never seen the Smith case as a racial issue," Sheriff Wells snapped with frustration as the thousandth reporter raised the question. "This is not like L.A. or Miami. Every incident is not automatically seized upon as racial. And that's a good thing."

His back up, Wells asserted that the good citizens of Union had better things to do than stage riots. He was dipping into treacherous waters. But the good name of his hometown was being maligned.

"Union's a quiet, God-fearing community. If you're looking for a good Christian community, a quiet community that hasn't progressed in many years, this is a good one," Wells added without a trace of irony.

But it was a slow news day, and reporters had to file something. In a pinch, the race issue made for a sexy story.

"If she had reported her kids taken by a Chinese, the police would be looking for a Chinese man," one local black minister said, defending the authorities. But the remark meant little. Union was very much a black-and-white community.

As far as Asians, Hispanics, or Native Americans are concerned, "You're pretty much talking about ones and twos around here," said Mac Johnston.

Reporters phoned black leaders from major cities, who were quick to respond with mildly incendiary comments about police treatment of blacks in general. It made Wells bristle. Suddenly it appeared as if, simply by inviting the nation into town, Union might be used as a pawn in a national race drama. Wells felt he had good reason to be defensive. How dare people try to rile things up?

McElroy Hughes was one local man who didn't buy the town cry of "All is well."

"These people have lived in a vacuum all their lives," Hughes says of his black neighbors. "They don't know what's out there. There's a lot of apathy in Union."

Hughes, fifty-eight, left Union in 1955 for New York City, where he worked for the city transit system. When he returned to his hometown in 1988, "I didn't see progress, I saw regress."

Hughes does not measure equality by the number of interracial couples walking the street. Nor does he rate harmony by the level of superficial peace. To Hughes, what people carry in their pockets and in their heads is far more significant.

The hard-fought battle for school integration had an unexpected downside. In the all-black schools of Hughes's day, students were instructed by the most talented black adults in the community. Now, he saw black children asea in schools where the majority of students, and nearly all the teachers, were white. Good grades, it turned out, cannot be legislated. Nor can the law dictate friendship.

"Blacks and whites see each other in the classroom," Hughes says. "The next time they see each other is on the football field."

In present-day Union, Hughes was confronted with what he viewed as a beaten-down population of blacks, poorer even than the folks he remembered from the '50s. Just as so many whites had fled, it seemed as if all the best and brightest blacks were gone.

"The most talented people left the state," says Hughes. "No one is going to stay in these conditions."

The numbers bear out Hughes's observations. In Union County, thirty-eight percent of all households fall below the federal poverty line, though the sting is mitigated somewhat by the area's lower-than-average cost of living. Still, blacks, on average, fare far worse than their white neighbors. According to 1989 figures, the average annual income for a white Union resident was a mere $10,939.

For blacks, the income figure was pegged at $6,711.

Mac Johnston attributes part of the disparity to the large number of black widows living on Social Security. But that does not account for it all. In September 1994, the county's total unemployment rate stood at 7.3 percent. For blacks, unemployment hovered around 10 percent.

Patterns of employment and income were set here long ago. And things don't change quickly in Union.

But things do improve, even here. Sometimes, that requires a little effort.

When Hughes returned to Union in 1988, he said, he was shocked to find that a black man minding his own business on Main Street was likely to be picked up by police for loitering, and charged a $100 fine. If he didn't have the money, he could be stuck in jail for up to five days. Hughes met the challenge by calling a meeting of city administrators and townspeople. Only about fifteen to twenty showed up. It was enough.

"This town is cursed," Hughes told them, "and it will remain cursed until we create a situation in which the black man is equal."

Black men no longer get jailed in Union for loitering, of that Hughes is fairly sure.

And in the autumn of 1994, as Hughes watched carefully, black men did not suffer undue harassment from police. Hughes received not one complaint from a black resident dissatisfied with the police investigation in the Smith boys' abduction. A remarkable statistic, even among a population that, according to Hughes, was filled with apathy.

The one matter relating to the investigation that most troubled the town's black population had nothing to do with the police, but with the smug outsiders who descended from up North. If the missing boys were black, some residents wondered, would the national media have considered the case such big news?

Fortunately, there was no way of telling. All of Union's black children were safely accounted for.

7

The Long Vigil

It's like throwing a rock in the water. Right afterward, you have ripples. Once they go away, it's hard to find where the rock was thrown.

—Union County Sheriff Howard Wells giving an analogy to illustrate the complete absence of clues in the disappearance of Michael and Alex Smith.

It was taking too long. Much too long.

As the weekend approached, police had received no demand for ransom in exchange for the safe return of Michael and Alex. The car was still missing. No carjacker was located. No one confessed.

Hundreds of volunteer searchers coordinated their efforts with hundreds of FBI and state police agents, sheriff's deputies, and local police. Thousands of tips were reported to authorities. Tens of thousands of dollars in reward money was posted by businesses in the Union area. Hundreds of thousands of flyers, signs, and yellow ribbons dotted the area. And still, it seemed as if Michael and Alex Smith were farther away from home than ever.

Sheriff Wells ceased trying to mask his frustration.

"We have dogs here at a moment's notice," he told reporters. "We've got a hostage rescue team at a moment's notice. We have aircraft that'll take us wherever we need to go. Right now, we're trying to do the impossible. We're trying to work a case without a crime scene."

This case defied all reason. The sheriff had at his disposal all the sophisticated equipment he could ask for. He had more manpower at his beck and call than he knew what to do with. In addition, the entire world was on the lookout for the little boys. Such abundant resources should be enough to put a dent in any case, particularly a kidnapping. The pressure alone should have been enough to force the hardest kidnapper to crack.

But three days after the Smith boys vanished, investigators were back to square one.

"We're interviewing family members, looking for a revenge motive," the sheriff allowed. "But so far this looks like a random act," he added carefully.

Still, the lack of any kind of evidence stymied the troops.

"It would be very hard to be lost in this county for a long time," said Wells. The woods were thick with deer hunters. "We've never looked for a car this long here that we haven't found."

Tips poured in so fast and furiously from around the globe, the FBI had to set up a computerized system at the Union courthouse to help organize the incoming data. It was a sorely needed addition. An astonishingly high number of urgent messages were imparted by fortune tellers and soothsayers eager to get into the act.

"A lot of our calls are coming from more of a psychic nature or people who are having visions and dreams, more so than sightings themselves," Wells said.

The most obvious crackpots were relegated to the back burner. Other tipsters were patiently interviewed by police. Even a certifiable kook, cops knew from experience, is capable of providing information valuable to solving a criminal case.

On Friday, October 28, the computer spit out two promising leads. It appeared the electronic tipsorter might have done the trick.

A car matching the description of Susan Smith's Mazda had been spotted at Shut-In Mountain in the neighboring state of Tennessee. It was a good place to ditch a hot car. On horseback and in helicopters, searchers hit the trail.

Meanwhile, closer to Union, a girl reported seeing a strange man emerge from the woods caked with mud. It was conceivable the carjacker had spent the last three days crouching in the brush. The account was enough to renew the search in and around the Sumter National Forest. Union County measured 515 square miles, much of it densely wooded. But with enough dogs, horses, people, and vehicles, there wasn't a space big enough to hide two children. Or so it seemed.

Susan and David fled from the spotlight. The constant police interviews, the incessant telephone calls from reporters, the TV cameras staked outside their homes proved overwhelming. Neither Susan nor David seemed to expect the case to grow this big. Or go on this long.

One man who thought he had something valuable to offer Susan Smith was Marc Klaas. In October 1993, Klaas's daughter, Polly, was snatched by a stranger from her suburban California bedroom, and murdered. As in the Smith case, Polly's plight received saturation coverage from the national media. Her death came to symbolize every parent's worst nightmare, the menace that has come to be known by the pithy phrase Stranger Danger. Since the tragedy, Klaas had devoted much of his time to helping parents in similar straits.

After the Smith case broke, Klaas flew to South Carolina, accompanied by a cognitive artist named Jeanne Boylan. Boylan has a background in psychology, and she hoped to unlock subtle details of the abductor's appearance from Susan's memory. Boylan was known for creating remarkably accurate police sketches from tiny specks of information, and her services were badly needed here. The only existing image of Susan's carjacker was so generic, it was nearly useless.

But Klaas and Boylan were not welcomed into the home at Mt. Vernon Estates, where Susan gathered with family and close friends. Five days in a row, Klaas knocked on the door. Five times, he was sent away.

At first, Klaas assumed his icy reception was due to the fact that his trip to Union was sponsored by the syndicated television show *American Journal*, which planned to produce a segment on the efforts of Boylan and Klaas. But Susan's absolute refusal to meet Klaas face-to-face baffled the man who had suffered so recently under similar circumstances. Certainly, he could have been of some help.

Susan would not budge, and Klaas eventually left her alone. How peculiar, thought artist Boylan, that a victim of such a heinous crime would feel threatened by the appearance of a grieving father and a woman professionally trained in psychology.

For the second night since Michael and Alex went missing, the temperature fell below freezing in rural South Carolina. The latest leads, like all those that came before, had turned to dust. Union residents shivered from more than the cold.

Saying they hoped it would help people identify the boys, Susan and David released to television stations a homemade videotape recorded during Alex's first birthday party. Alex turned one on August 5, a Friday. His mother threw him a little shindig at home two days later, on a sweltering Sunday afternoon.

In the video, the towheaded birthday boy looks so cheerful, all decked out in light-blue overalls and a blue short-sleeved shirt. Alex is all smiles as he waves his little hands in the air, trying to help his mother open a large pile of beautifully wrapped presents. Many of the boxes are bigger than he is.

Susan is seen sitting cross-legged on the floor wearing shorts and a light-blue sleeveless blouse, her hair tied up in a young girl's white bow.

"Look!" Susan coos to Alex, while showing him the greeting card that came with a gift.

"Who's this?"

Michael, ever-protective of his little brother, helps Alex maneuver his way through the booty. Michael gently pushes as Alex sits high in the driver's seat of a new plastic kiddie car. The tot's legs are still too small to propel the vehicle.

In another scene, the guest of honor sits in his yellow high chair, with a red helium-filled balloon tied to its back. Alex pokes his tiny fingers curiously along the perimeter of a white sheet cake that's bordered with a ribbon of blue-and-purple frosting. Once again, Michael is close to his side. He presents his brother with a small, plastic pinwheel, slipping the gift carefully into Alex's birthday cake.

At one year old, the world was an exciting, miraculous place. Alex had so much to look forward to.

The images of the children's exuberant faces, the boys' tender interactions, tugged at the heartstrings in ways Susan's plaintive cries could not begin to match. It was impossible to get those faces out of your mind.

Were they somewhere safe and warm? Perhaps they were being cared for by a loving couple who went to great lengths to find children of their own. Folks had heard about childless couples who paid good money for children, no questions asked. The alternatives were too appalling to consider. And too difficult to dismiss.

Suddenly, the woods no longer seemed filled with catfish ponds and deer, but with depraved men capable of doing unspeakable things to a child. Better not to think.

But as the nights grew colder, the imagination strayed. Please God, they prayed, if the boys have to die, just let it be quick.

The people of Union were losing hope. They needed strength to make it through another night. And for that, they looked to the church.

Sundays always drew a crowd, but nothing like this. The authorities had tried everything—sonar, radar, psychics, and TV. It was time for the people to seek help from on high.

The crowd packed the pews of Buffalo United Methodist Church, where Susan and David were regular attendees.

"Look for a merciful God to deliver us," the Rev. Mark Long prayed.

In the evening, candles illuminated the inky banks of John D. Long Lake, as hundreds gathered for prayer vigils. Parents hugged the necks of small children, realizing fully, for maybe the first time, just how precious they were.

If the power of prayer couldn't deliver the boys home, at least it might keep Union's spirits from falling. The churches were crammed with neighbors, black and white. They prayed together and together they cried, their tears flowing into one, unified river. In the 200 years since the city was named Union, the name had never seemed so deserved.

If only things could stay that way.

8

Turning Point

The joys of parents are secret; and so are their griefs and fears; they cannot utter the one; nor they will not utter the other. Children sweeten labors; but they make misfortunes more bitter.

—Francis Bacon, *Essays*, 1597.

"Is your name Susan Smith?"

"Yes."

Susan fidgeted nervously as the operator strapped her arm to the polygraph machine. The questioner's even, emotionless voice was unnerving. The correct answers to his initial questions were so obvious, they made the entire exercise seem idiotic.

"Do you live at 407 Toney Road?"

The FBI introduced the lie-detector device at the end of the first week of the Smith boys' disappearance. Three days after a kidnapping was a longer gap than most experts recommended before authorities should test the parents. "Put the family on the polygraph right away," says Ruben Rodriguez, senior analyst for the National Center for Missing and Exploited Children. "Eliminate them very quickly or implicate them."

But this was no typical case. Sheriff Wells reassured Susan that he believed her story. This was just FBI procedure, she was not the suspect. Please Susan, investigators said, we need your cooperation. We've got to rule you out, once and for all.

Susan agreed to take the test. She did not request to have an attorney present. In fact, during her long days of questioning, the subject of a lawyer never came up. That would make Susan look guilty. She insisted she had nothing to hide.

Since the abduction, Susan was an emotional wreck. That only made her more confident she'd be able to beat the polygraph. Jangled nerves can bollix up the results. Besides, Susan was a convincing liar, even under duress. She'd told her carjacking story so many times, even she was beginning to believe it.

Susan had another reason to relax: Polygraph readings are open to highly subjective interpretations. It was possible for two polygraph experts to read the same test and draw completely opposite conclusions about the subject's sincerity. That's why lie-detector test results are rarely admissible in court.

"Are you married to David Smith?"

Susan was asked to sit still. The machine to which she was attached contained a variety of sensors, each designed to measure minute variations in Susan's pulse as she answered a battery of questions with a "Yes" or a "No." Hooked up to the sensors were a series of pens that left trails as a roll of paper moved beneath them. Each time Susan opened her mouth, her reply set in motion a chorus of jerking pens. As the paper slid under them, each implement left in its wake a wavy line. Authorities hoped the scribbling pens would draw a road map of Susan's mind.

They asked her to lie.

"Is your shirt blue?"

"Yes."

The operator checked the size and shape of the wave that resulted when Susan knowingly told a lie. Once the device was calibrated against the unique trail created by Susan's answers, the polygraph machine was up and ready to go.

Susan had already described the carjacking countless times. Day after day, she was taken to various civic buildings around Union, where Sheriff Wells and SLED Chief Robert Stewart were joined by some of the most experienced law-enforcement agents in South Carolina and beyond. Charlie Webber. Sandy Templeton. Eddie Harris. Former Sheriff William Jolly. Eventually Pete Logan, one of SLED's most senior investigators, was summoned to help confront the mother.

Each time, they asked many of the same questions. They wanted to know if Susan had enemies. If she owed money. They asked about the state of her marriage, and her state of mind. Some of the men interrogating Susan had defused hostage situations. They'd broken down the guard of some of the toughest criminals in the state. If Susan were hiding something, they were the right people to pluck it out of her.

On more than one occasion, Susan looked as if she had something new to say.

During one session, Susan put her head on the table in front of her. She looked weary. She grew silent. She was thinking. Everybody in the room held his breath.

Susan's mannerisms were familiar to the investigators. Hers was the look of a cornered criminal. After all the hours spent under interrogation, Susan appeared ready to give up.

But she didn't confess. After each such interlude, she recovered and sat up straight. Gathering the remains of her original resolve, Susan returned to her story of the red light, the carjacker, and the kids.

The polygraph test, however, did not afford Susan any dramatic license. "Yes" and "No" were the only acceptable replies. She could tell no tales. She was instructed to sit stock-still.

"Do you have sons named Michael and Alex?"

In this stilted manner, Susan repeated the tale.

The polygraph operator interspersed pertinent questions among his queries about such things as eye color and name. Whether the subject was the weather or the size of the carjacker's gun, he never altered the tone of his cool, even voice. He didn't need to. The wavy lines would judge Susan's storytelling ability.

"Do you know where the children are?"

Susan did not hesitate.

"No."

Susan was right about one thing. Her frazzled nerves helped bollix the machine. At the conclusion of the test, the polygraph expert rendered his opinion. The results, he said, were "inconclusive." To a woman who hoped the polygraph might help clear her name, this was not the most desirable judgment.

But then, things got worse.

Portions of the test were not so muddy. In fact, the expert was certain of their value. One question in particular leaped out at the polygraph interpreter:

"Do you know where the children are?"

"No."

There was only one way to read the wavy lines. They spelled the word *liar*.

Susan knew damn well where those children were.

News leaks can be as useful to law-enforcement as squad cars and guns. But they are far trickier to manage. A potentially explosive story appears in the newspaper, usually attributed to an anonymous "source close to the investigation." A flurry of publicity follows the revelation, and a high-ranking police spin master steps forward to set the record straight. He might deny the story outright. More likely, he'll say he has "no knowledge" of the information reported.

Occasionally, the person issuing the denial is the same person who leaked the story.

Sometimes, stories leak unintentionally. Even a cop can have a big mouth. Often, though, they occur when someone high up wants a story made public. When he wants to turn up the heat on a suspect.

Whatever the motive, the person who leaked the story of Susan Smith's lie-detector test made a colossal impact on the case. In an instant, public opinion took a 180-degree turn. Suddenly, it was as if the world's saddest mother had an indelible question mark painted on her face.

The polygraph test was front-page news. On Saturday, October 29, two South Carolina newspapers, *The State*, based in Columbia, and *The Greenville News* reported that Susan "failed" the test. Meanwhile, in North Carolina, *The Charlotte Observer* reported that the test results were "inconclusive." None of the three papers obtained the exact questions

Susan was asked. Still, each newspaper's account was accurate, if incomplete.

Until this moment, if anyone harbored doubts about Susan's story, he'd never dare utter a discouraging word in public. Now, those involved in the case didn't have to worry. The media would assume the role of Susan's chief skeptics.

"Serious questions" have emerged about the Susan Smith kidnapping case, television stations and wire services reported dutifully. In other accounts, a more brutal word was floated for public consideration. Was the kidnapping a hoax?

Around Union, the whispers started in earnest. The same people who for five days had studied the profiles of black men now gradually shifted their stares to Susan's pale face. There was much talk about Susan's impending divorce. About her various boyfriends, some real, some invented. Word spread of her fits in Winn-Dixie. And of her breakdowns.

While the gossip mongers had a field day, others in Union closed ranks around Susan. The reports, they protested, were exaggerated and cruel. Hadn't she suffered enough? Besides, Susan Smith just wasn't the type of person capable of doing something awful. Everyone knew that.

"She's such a nice girl," insisted one neighbor after another. "Such a good mother."

Alice Valentine, who lives next door to the Smith house in Toney Road, would hear none of this speculation:

"There is no way you can convince me that she had anything to do with those babies' disappearance.

"Her and David are such nice people. They were so friendly."

There was that word again: Nice. In the rural South, being nice is more than a virtue. It is an alibi.

Then again, not to everyone.

Catherine Frost, who lives across the street from the Smiths' house, was not completely swayed by Susan's story. Though she'd always liked Susan, Frost was an extremely observant neighbor and involved citizen. Frost followed crime reports on a police scanner she kept in the bedroom.

The details of the carjacking, as overheard on the scanner, struck this amateur crime buff as odd. For one thing, why would a kidnapper dump the mother so close to a house whose lights were on? If the man was frantic to escape, why leave Susan in a place where she'd have no trouble summoning immediate help?

Susan's story didn't add up. But other things did. Lately, Frost noticed that shortly before the kidnapping, a man other than David started dropping by Susan's house regularly. His visits lasted for what seemed an inordinately long time.

Frost told the FBI about Susan's gentleman caller. The tale was not received as idle tattling. The tidbit would help authorities develop a new picture of Susan. As Frost worded it, Susan's mournful expression as she clung to her husband could be nothing more than an elaborate put-on.

Meanwhile, over at Mt. Vernon Estates, the mood was grim. For five days, Susan and David moaned and prayed in each other's arms amid an ever-expanding collection of friends and family members. Susan's mother and stepfather, Linda and Beverly Russell, cleared a spot in the garage where they placed a large, tan couch. Visitors drove up and parked in the driveway, then walked over to the open garage area. There, they could enjoy the fresh air while shielded from prying eyes in the street.

As word of the polygraph spread to the Russells'

garage, Susan was beside herself. She was a victim. It was unfair to accuse her.

When he wasn't questioning Susan, Sheriff Wells was comforting her. A regular visitor to Mt. Vernon Estates, Wells cried with the family and offered emotional support. Now, he instructed them to ignore media reports. Things like that just happen, he shrugged. There was nothing anyone could do.

They took him at his word.

"We didn't believe anything in the media," said Susan's brother, Scotty Vaughan.

As for David, he pulled Susan a little nearer, and gently brushed the tendrils from her forehead. Never before had Susan needed him so desperately. Maybe that's what had been missing in their marriage.

In their hour of agony, Susan and David grew closer than ever. Never for an instant did David doubt his wife.

For Sheriff Wells, the news leaks complicated an already tense situation. Previously, when reporters asked why he was questioning the family, Wells danced around the matter by saying simply, "We have to rule everything out."

But now, the eyes of the world were trained on Susan. Wells wasn't the kind of man to tell a bald-faced lie. Even the Justice Department's manual on kidnapping encouraged honesty with reporters. But the manual also warned that cases can veer out of control if the media makes too many potentially harmful assumptions. And Wells feared he was losing his handle on this one.

He tried his hand at spinning.

"We're trying to corroborate her story, because not only is she the victim in this case but the public is trying to make her the suspect," Wells said.

Never mind that Susan already was a suspect.

Wells did his best to blame police interest in Susan on the media.

"Do not read into our contacts with her as laying blame. She's our only witness."

In this backhanded manner, Wells confirmed that a parallel investigation was being conducted. But he would not confirm the polygraph story.

"Naturally, people are going to speculate," Wells said, by way of defending Susan. "People automatically assume things when an investigation goes on this long."

It did not help matters that on Saturday, the search for the boys all but halted. The weekend brought deer hunters in droves to Sumter National Forest. Helicopters equipped with heat-seeking devices continued to buzz the treetops. But on Saturday, no one wandered through the forest, calling out the names Michael and Alex. That was a good way to get shot.

The story got more publicity Saturday night, as the Fox television network program *America's Most Wanted* devoted a segment to the Smith boys. Over the years, the show has been instrumental in solving many police riddles.

First, a dramatization of the carjacking was presented, as Susan reported it. Then a phone number was provided for viewers to call with information that might be helpful in solving the case. After the show aired, switchboards were again flooded with tips.

It seemed impossible that a pile that big did not contain one, single useful clue.

But on Sunday, October 31, detectives decided the nationwide search was unwieldy and pointless. The investigation was right back to where it started.

For a second time, divers plunged into the crisp

waters of John D. Long Lake, and probed the bottom for a car. Searchers on horseback returned to the spot where Susan reported her Mazda stolen.

"We're back to ground zero," Sheriff Wells announced. "I think there's a possibility they could be in Union."

What are they doing? Members of Susan's and David's families complained among themselves when they saw that the probe again was focused close to home.

"I wondered why they weren't out there, looking for the children," said David's mother, Barbara Benson, who arrived in Union over the weekend.

"It seemed wrong that they were back in Union."

"We can only hope and pray that the man who took our precious babies from us can find it somewhere in his heart to return them safely. No one can understand the pain we are going through—how much harder it gets with each day that goes by without them being here."

On Monday, November 1, Susan and David broke the silence of several days. Susan's cousin, Margaret Gregory, thirty-one, read their statement from a sheet of paper outside Union's courthouse. By her side stood Sheriff Wells.

Part of the message was directed to Michael and Alex:

"We have put our faith and trust in the Lord that he is taking care of you both. And hopefully soon you will be back home with Mommy and Daddy.

"You both have to be brave and you must hold on to each other because we are doing everything in our power to get you back home where you belong."

Six days after the boys were taken, Susan evoked

the name of the Lord. With suspicion mounting that her carjacking tale might be a fabrication, it was high time she started praying.

Gregory told the assembled crowd that Susan and David didn't have the emotional strength to deliver their statement personally. So it was up to Gregory to brush aside questions about the rumors of a hoax.

"We are concentrating on what we have to do to bring these children back home. Rumors are exactly that—rumors."

But rumors have a way of multiplying. And the family's concentration was about to be broken.

On Monday night, the syndicated TV show *A Current Affair* aired a genuine scoop. The show introduced America to Mitchell Sinclair, the millworker Susan had said she was going to visit on the night Michael and Alex vanished. It was revealed that Susan changed her story to police about her intended destination on the night of the kidnapping—another straw in the mounting stack of Susan's inconsistent statements.

That was alarming enough. But one comment made by Mitch hit the airwaves like cannon fire:

"The truth will come out."

To some ears, it was as good as a confession. Mitch seemed to know a great deal about this case—more, perhaps, than the authorities. Union went wild with rumors about Susan and Mitch. Were they in on the kidnapping together? Or had Susan told Mitch what she did with the children, and asked him to cover for her? On the most superficial level, a liaison between the two seemed plausible. In many ways, Susan had a lot more in common with Mitch Sinclair than she did with her husband.

In high school, Mitch, with his thick glasses and

winning smile, was a joiner, like Susan. He was an honor student who belonged to all the clubs, and he wasn't afraid of playing the fool for a laugh. The Union High School yearbook for 1988 contains a photograph of Mitch dressed up in a bouffant wig and evening gown—his costume in the competition for homecoming king. All the guys in the contest pranced around in drag. Mitch came in as a finalist.

Mitch was engaged to Susan's best friend, Donna Garner, so Susan and Mitch were often seen keeping company. Of course, to some people that spelled adultery. Hey, it was a way of life in Union. It didn't help matters that Sheriff Wells was so intrigued by Mitch Sinclair's TV debut. Already Mitch had submitted to a polygraph test, and he was ruled out as a suspect. Or so he thought.

"I think we have more to talk about," the sheriff said menacingly.

As it turned out, the entire quote uttered by Mitch on *A Current Affair* wasn't as damaging as it first appeared.

"The truth will come out . . . and that is just like the sheriff says it is," Mitch had said.

After a few more questions, Wells was convinced there was nothing more to the Mitch story. It would take a while longer to persuade the rest of Union, not to mention the world, that Mitch Sinclair was not involved in the kidnapping.

What the public did not know at the time was that investigators had dumped Mitch, and now focused squarely on another man in Susan's life. They were certain this new man, not Mitch, was their magic key to the truth.

Investigators took a trip to the offices of Conso Products. Their arrival raised no alarm; Susan worked at Conso as a secretary. But on this occasion, detectives weren't there to examine Susan's work-space, or to talk to her boss. Their appointment was with Tom Findlay, the head of the graphics depart-ment and the son of Conso owner J. Cary Findlay. A friend of Tom's had tipped off cops that young Findlay had something in his computer they might find fascinating.

At their request, Findlay switched on his com-puter terminal. With a few taps of the keyboard, he located a file. A few more taps, and the office printer clicked into motion.

Findlay ripped a sheet of paper from the printer and handed it to detectives. They read it quickly, then hurried back to headquarters.

The letter was dated Tuesday, October 18, a week before the kidnapping. It was addressed to Susan Smith.

It's over.

In the note, Findlay listed a number of reasons why he was cutting Susan loose. But like Susan, investigators saw only one: Findlay didn't want to raise her kids.

It was like finding the Rosetta stone. For the first time since this maddening case began, everything made sense.

9

The Noose

There is nothing so powerful as truth—and often nothing so strange.

—Daniel Webster, *Argument on the Murder of Captain White*, 1830.

"It is a nightmare that seems to have no end."

On the one-week anniversary of Michael and Alex's disappearance, Susan and David turned up the volume. Again, Susan's cousin, Margaret Gregory, served as their mouthpiece.

"We can't feed them, we can't wipe away their tears, we can't hold them, we can't hug them," Gregory read from a sheet of paper outside Union's courthouse.

"The hardest part of all is not knowing where they are. It is torture."

The couple prepared a message for the children, as well.

"You both have to be brave and you must hold onto each other because we are doing everything in our power to get you home where you belong.

"We love you!"

The Smiths worked hard to deflect attention from Susan, and turn it back to the children. Reporters, however, didn't take the hint. In pursuit of the story, they were relentless.

"They try to avoid listening to a lot of the innuendo that has been in the media," Gregory replied to the scores of questions about Susan's conflicting statements to police.

Sheriff Wells was spinning his own statements so fast, he nearly lost his balance. The sheriff suggested that the widely reported inconsistencies in Susan's stories might be the result of stress or medication.

"I don't know what happened in this case, but I'm treating it as a carjacking that happened as it was reported," Wells said, presenting half of the truth.

In the next breath, the sheriff gave a glimpse of the other half:

"We're looking at everything. Nothing has been ruled out."

The intensity of the investigators' focus on Susan was getting nearly impossible for Wells to explain away. Detectives were seen searching Susan's house Tuesday. News of a second polygraph spread like wildfire.

Do you know where the children are?

The second test was administered by South Carolina officials. The drill was the same as when the FBI ran the show. Susan's "Yes" and "No" questions varied somewhat, but they covered the same ground. As with her first polygraph, the overall test results were deemed "inconclusive."

Also this time, portions of the test were crystal clear.

"Do you know where the children are?" Susan was asked.

"No," she replied.

Whether the polygraph was administered by the feds or the state, Susan could not wiggle out of that question on the basis of fractured nerves. The polygraph saw through her deception. The noose was tightening around Susan's neck.

Something exciting happened before dawn Wednesday. Authorities saw it as the break they had waited for. Alex Smith was apparently found, all the way on the West Coast. No one was sure how he got there, or with whom. The important thing was that the boy was alive. Or so it seemed.

On the night of Tuesday, November 1, a desk clerk at the Black Angus Motor Inn in Seattle called local police. The clerk reported that a baby boy was abandoned at the inn. When cops arrived, clerks told them that a white man driving a car with South Carolina license plates had checked into the motel on Monday, Halloween night. With him was his son, who was about fourteen months old. The man called the child Zack.

"He asked about the care and feeding of a little boy," said clerk Teri Lewis. Rather a curious question from a father on the road with his own baby.

The man, who said he was from Charleston, told motel personnel on Tuesday that he needed to run a few errands. He asked desk clerk Linda Martinez to baby-sit his son.

By nightfall, the father was nowhere to be found.

The baby was placed with Seattle's Child Protection Services, where someone noticed how closely Baby Doe matched the description of little

Alex Smith. The Smith boys' pictures by now had been displayed in every city of every state in the country.

The call from Seattle came into Union after midnight Wednesday morning. Investigators were cool; too many attractive leads had turned into dead-ends. But after several conversations with the West Coast, this tip shot to the top of the pile. Wells could not contain his optimism.

"It is a very promising lead right now," the sheriff said Wednesday. "It could provide us with the break we needed."

The man's inept behavior around the baby seemed a dead giveaway that he wasn't really the father. Besides, a father wouldn't abandon his son, now would he? The South Carolina plates on the man's car clinched it. What's more, the boy sure looked like Alex.

"If you looked at the comparison photos, you have to look for a second to see if there is a difference," said Seattle police spokesman Sean O'Donnell.

Once again, however, looks proved deceiving. He was someone else's child.

While little Zack's parents indeed hailed from South Carolina, his mother had moved to Seattle some time back. The man at the motor inn turned out really to be the child's father, who came to town to visit the mother and son. His errands apparently took longer than expected.

The disappointment was crushing. Eight days had gone by without a clue.

"It's very hard when you get your hopes up and see them dashed," Wells said.

But the sheriff recovered his bearings quickly.

"I'm of the belief now that this is not going to affect our case," Wells said in classic cryptic style. "It doesn't lead me to believe the case is not going to be solved."

The next item on the agenda was to find a new headquarters; the investigative team had outgrown its room in the Union courthouse. Their new home would have to be close by, however, because probers again were concentrating on Union County.

This time, they planned to stay put in Union, said the sheriff, "until we're led otherwise."

Onlookers were perplexed by the return to Union. If there really was a carjacker, why the heck would he still be in town? What was the sheriff hiding?

"First of all, I would like to say to whoever has my children that they please, I mean please, bring 'em home to us where they belong."

Smoked out of hiding by negative publicity, Susan collected her wits sufficiently to face her media accusers—the ones who now referred to the case as an "alleged kidnapping."

The stated goal of the press conference was twofold: The Smiths wanted to keep the children's plight in the public eye, and they also wanted to make an appeal to the carjacker's conscience by showing him the kind of people they are.

Susan had other motives she didn't care to mention. Her hold on the case was slipping, and she felt the need to bring public sympathy back on her side.

On Wednesday, November 2, Susan stood before the courthouse in eyeglasses and ponytail, David next to her. With touching devotion, David put his arm around his wife protectively. They hugged whenever Susan gave the signal.

Still dry-eyed, but obviously imbued with grief, Susan improved her message and honed her delivery since that first, shaky outing with the press. Susan still gazed downward, however, as she addressed the throng about her missing sons.

"Our lives have been torn apart by this tragic event," she said. "I can't express how much they are wanted back home, how much we love 'em, we miss 'em.

"They—they are our heart and who . . . " Susan faltered, then collected herself.

"I have prayed every day and there's not one minute that goes by that I don't think about these boys. And I have prayed that whoever has 'em, that the Lord will let them—let him realize that they are missed and loved more than any children in this world, and that whoever has 'em, I—I pray every day that you're takin' care of 'em, and know that we will do anything—anything—we will, to help you to get 'em home, back to us.

"I just can't express it enough that we just got to get 'em home. That's just where they belong, with their mama and daddy."

Some things about Susan's performance had not changed. As before, Susan's words centered on herself—on *her* feelings about the children, *her* despair over the kidnapping. At least this time, she bothered to mention the boys, as well as the Lord.

Next, it was David's turn at the microphone. Unlike Susan, David did not use the opportunity to discuss his own pain. Rather, he appealed to everyone in earshot to help find his sons. Unlike his wife, David stared directly into the cameras as he spoke.

"I would like to take the time to plead to the American public that you please do not give up on these two little boys or the search for their safe return home to us. That you continue to look for this car, these two—our children, and for the suspect himself. That you continue to keep your eyes open and anything that you see that might could help, to please call and let it be known.

"We ask that you continue to pray for me and my wife and for our family. But most of all, that you continue to pray—the American public continue to pray for Michael and Alex, that they are returned home safely to their mother and father and the family members who love them so much. That you pray most of all for them and that they are being taken care of and that they are safe. And that they will return home safely."

Susan would not be upstaged. Continuing in David's vein, she chimed in:

"I want to say to my babies"—here, Susan managed a sob—"that your mama loves you so much, and your daddy—this whole family loves you so much. And you guys have got to be strong because you are—we—we—I just know, I just feel in my heart that you're OK. But you've got to take care of each other, and your mama and daddy are going to be right here waitin' on you when you get home. I love you so much."

David echoed: "We love you."

Susan was on a roll. The spotlight cast a flattering glow on the young mother, and Susan had always enjoyed attention. Even in a crisis, she could not resist bringing the focus back to herself.

"I want to tell a story," she began. "The night that this happened, before I left my house that night, Michael did somethin' that he's never done before. He had his pooper [pacifier] in his mouth and he came up to me and he took his pooper out, and he put his arms around me and he told me, 'I love you so much, Mama.'

"And he—he's always told me he loved me, but

never before, not without me telling him first. And that was just—I am holdin' on to that so much 'cause it just means so much.

"I love 'em. I—I—I just can't say, express enough, I have been to the Lord in prayers every day with my family and by myself, with my husband.

"It just seems so unfair that somebody could take two such beautiful children and, I don't understand. I—I have put all my trust and faith in the Lord, that He's taking care of 'em, and that He will bring them home to us.

"That's all. I can't—I don't want to say anything else."

It's little wonder David never was able to please Susan during their marriage. While he was naturally reticent, Susan had a flair for drama and craved attention like a drug. Now, in their hour of mutual suffering, David let Susan take over. Sublimating his own needs, he offered his wife the unconditional support she always demanded.

Susan Smith went to extreme lengths to thoroughly domesticate her husband. Then again, she usually found a way to get what she wanted.

The nationally televised performance proved dazzling. People who had doubted Susan started coming back around to her side. She'd achieved her goal. However, not everyone was so favorably impressed.

After the press conference, investigators returned to the house on Toney Road. This time, their search was more than cursory. They dusted for fingerprints, and removed a batch of bags. They even combed through a crawl space in the basement.

On the same day, Susan was questioned for hours. *Tell us again how it happened.*

A live press conference. The thorough search. Hours of grilling. Rougher customers than Susan had yielded under far less pressure. But Susan stood her ground. As a suspect, she was in a league of her own.

Susan kept it up.

"I was running around my house yesterday morning all excited. I really thought they had found one of my children. And when I got to the courthouse and found that lead had disintegrated, I was very devastated."

Thursday morning, November 3, Susan and David met the nation, live, via satellite, on two morning television shows. Over breakfast, people coast-to-coast watched the couple hold hands. Affixed to their chests were pictures of Michael and Alex, adorned by yellow ribbons.

On the CBS program *This Morning*, Susan affected just the right tone of wounded indignation when asked about reports that she might be lying about the carjacking.

"I did not have anything to do with the abduction of my children," she said without blinking.

"I don't think any parent could love their children any more than I do, and I would never even think about doing anything that would harm them. It's really very painful to have the finger pointed at you when it's your children involved."

On NBC's *Today* show, Susan played shamelessly to her fellow mothers in the audience.

"I was thinking last night, as a mother, it's only a natural instinct to protect your children from any harm, and the hardest part of this whole ordeal is not knowing if your children are getting what they need to survive. And it hurts real bad to have that protection barrier broken between parent and child.

"But I have put my faith in the Lord, and I really

believe that He's taking care of them. And they're too beautiful and precious that He's not going to let anything happen to them.

"And, Michael and Alex, I love you. And we're going to have the biggest celebration when you get home."

Had things turned out differently, Susan would have had a rosy future in politics. Dripping with sincerity, she bowled over many a skeptical viewer. She was so young and so maternal. And so very, very sad. No way somebody like that could harm her own kids.

After nine days, Susan's plan was working. She had perfected her storytelling. Her family stood by her. David believed in her. The investigators had no hard evidence to nail her. Eventually, they'd have to give up.

Maybe she'd remarry. Unencumbered by children, Susan could start her life anew with the richest man in town. She was young enough to have plenty more kids. Only later, when he was ready.

Or perhaps she and David would continue their lives together. Things between them had grown so sweet lately. Besides, without two children to raise, their salaries would go that much farther.

Susan was ready to spend her life as the world's most sympathetic former mother. It seemed as if she could go on this way forever.

She'd worn everybody down.

Sheriff Wells had reached his limit. For nine long days, Susan played him like a violin. He'd comforted her, cried with her, told her he believed her incredible story. The Mr. Nice Guy routine was wearing mighty thin.

It was later reported—inaccurately—that on

Thursday, November 3, Sheriff Wells marched Susan into a church. Under the eyes of Jesus, the sheriff was said to have "bluffed" Susan into believing that he was about to go public with her countless lies. In fact, the media never did get a full grasp as to what exactly transpired between Susan and Howard Wells on that fateful Thursday.

Here, then, is what happened, as revealed by a law-enforcement source:

Sheriff Wells met Susan at around 3 P.M. Thursday for another round of questioning. While they did drive to a church, they did not enter the building. Rather, Susan was led into a recreation center located behind the church. The idea was not to scare Susan with hell and damnation, but to take her to a quiet, secluded spot where the media could not find them.

Once inside the rec center, the sheriff did not *bluff* Susan. Instead, he told her the honest-to-God truth.

"We've called the national media into Union. We're gonna have to tell them everything."

Sheriff Wells is not the kind of man to play games. He was dead serious about his intention to throw Susan to the wolves. He had already covered for her way too long.

Wells had asked the media to follow this story. Now, reporters were forced to go on half-truths and suppositions, on rumors and innuendo. The media were invited guests, called in to help solve a crisis. Now it was time to level with the press.

Wells reviewed the list of problems with Susan's carjacking story:

- The traffic light at the deserted intersection in Monarch that couldn't possibly have been red, as Susan reported.

- Susan's fib about spending three hours shopping at Wal-Mart.
- Her claim to be on her way to visit Mitch Sinclair, when he in fact was not home.
- Her obvious deception after two polygraph examiners asked, "Do you know where the children are?"
- Tom Findlay's "Dear John" letter.

The list went on. There were dozens of minor inconsistencies, conflicting statements, and outright falsehoods.

"We have to tell them now," the sheriff told Susan. At that moment, Howard Wells was prepared to go straight to the courthouse, step up to the microphone, and read his list aloud.

To Susan, the threat was more than horrifying. Sheriff Wells was about to expose her as a liar, and worse. It didn't matter whether anyone could prove she was involved in the kidnapping. For the rest of her life, people would stare and whisper. She would be an outcast, a leper. Her mask would be torn off.

To Susan Smith, that was a fate worse than death.

The truth came rushing out of Susan in torrents. As Wells listened, she told it all.

Susan said she was upset, frantic, a "mental case" on the night of October 25. She was in love, but the man of her dreams wanted out of the relationship.

It's over.

So she took a drive, with Michael and Alex buckled into their car seats. The windows and doors were shut against the evening chill.

Lock the doors, Mama!

As she drove into the night, Susan ran through her options: Suicide, homicide. At the edge of John D. Long Lake, she made her choice.

Shut up, or I'll kill you.

She got out of the car.

The babies *wanted* her. They *needed* her. But Susan was in too big a hurry. The Mazda was rolling down the boat ramp. There wasn't enough time to unbuckle car seats. Susan had to move on.

Don't worry, I'll take care of them.

Now, look closely at the sketch of the black carjacker. Lighten the complexion and narrow the lips. The face in the picture belongs to Susan Smith.

10
Unnatural Acts

How a mother can kill her two children, fourteen months and three years, in the hopes that her boyfriend would like her is just a sign of how sick the system is, and I think people want to change. The only way you get change is to vote Republican.

—U.S. Representative Newt Gingrich, R-Georgia, in an interview with the Associated Press, November 5, 1994. Three days later, Republicans swept Congress in the mid-term election.

Suddenly, there was no place to hide.

The layers fell away like autumn leaves in the forest. Union's pleasant exterior loosened its grip, exposing the gnarled and ugly truth within.

November moved on, and lengthening shadows devoured the town's endless summer. Promises of idle porch conversation, of warm breezes and children's laughter, dissolved into cold and scary nights.

Nothing had changed, yet everything looked different. Churches that offered refuge from a world moving too fast were revealed to be filled with adulterers; the stores' shelves stocked with quiet desperation. Tidy shutters closed tightly on families wracked by divorce, incest, insanity. Small-town blandness never seemed so sinister. Union never looked so old.

The lake, scene of lazy days and moonlit nights, was a mirror, still. Its placid surface cast a flattering reflection back on all it surveyed, careful to reveal nothing of the secrets lurking below.

At the edge of sleep, children fended off vague and horrible demons that formed in the night out of familiar shapes. But now, there was no consoling them. The monster was real. All the world had seen her face.

The mother's smile, so warm and soothing, peeled away like the mask it always was. Beneath the sensuous, upturned lips lay a perverse grimace, an expression of pain and rage so great, its only means of survival was to destroy.

For twenty-three years, the beast lived right there among them. They just couldn't see.

Someone handed Susan a pen and paper.

"When I left my home on Tuesday, Oct. 25, I was very emotionally distraught. I didn't want to live anymore! I felt like things could never get any worse. When I left home, I was going to ride around a little while and then go to my mom's.

"As I rode and rode and rode, I felt even more anxiety coming upon me about not wanting to live. I felt I couldn't be a good mom anymore, but I didn't want my children to grow up without a mom. I felt I had to end our lives to protect us from any grief or harm.

"I had never felt so lonely and so sad in my entire life. I was in love with someone very much, but he didn't love me and never would. I could see why he could never love me.

"When I was at John D. Long Lake, I had never felt so scared and unsure as I did then. I wanted to end my life so bad and was in my car ready to go down that ramp into the water, and I did go part way, but I stopped. I went again and stopped. I then got out of the car and stood by the car a nervous wreck.

"Why was I feeling this way? Why was everything so bad in my life? I had no answers to these questions. I dropped to the lowest point when I allowed my children to go down that ramp into the water without me.

"I took off running and screaming 'Oh God! Oh God, no! What have I done? Why did you let this happen?' I wanted to turn around so bad and go back, but I knew it was too late. I was an absolute mental case! I couldn't believe what I had done.

"I love my children, with all my heart [Susan represents the word *heart* with a little drawing]. That will never change. I have prayed to them for forgiveness and hope that they will find it in their heart [another picture] to forgive me. I never meant to hurt them!! I am *sorry* for what has happened and I know that I need some help. I don't think I will ever be able to forgive myself for what I have done.

"My children, Michael and Alex, are with our Heavenly Father now, and I know that they will never be hurt again. As a mom, that means more than words could ever say.

"I knew from day one, the truth would prevail, but I was so scared I didn't know what to do. It was very tough emotionally to sit and watch my family hurt like they did. It was time to bring a peace of mind to everyone, including myself.

"My children deserve to have the best, and now they will. I broke down on Thursday, Nov. 3, and told Sheriff Howard Wells the truth. It wasn't easy, but after the truth was out, I felt like the world was lifted off my shoulders.

"I know now that it is going to be a tough and long road ahead of me. At this very moment, I don't feel I will be able to handle what's coming, but I have prayed to God that he give me the strength to survive each day and to face those times and situations in my life that will be extremely painful. I have put my total faith in God, and he will take care of me."

Susan penned her statement in the same neat, schoolgirl print she used three years earlier to express delight over Michael's birth in her album, "Baby's Milestones." Just as she had when her baby was born, Susan drew little doodles of hearts to represent feelings of love for her sons, now certainly dead.

The confession, spanning two handwritten pages, was signed Susan V. Smith, and dated 11/3/94. The last page was signed by two witnesses, an agent from the FBI and another from SLED.

Howard Wells was numb. The moment he'd waited for so long had arrived. But there was no joy in the rec room after Susan spilled her guts. It was impossible that Michael and Alex survived what Susan did to them. She killed her own children. They weren't coming back.

Wells asked Susan if there was anything she wanted. It was clear she wasn't going home any time soon.

"I'm sorry. I'm so very sorry," Susan whimpered, over and over.

She did have one request.

"Please tell my family I'm sorry," Susan begged. "Tell them I still love them, and I hope they still love me."

It was a pathetic spectacle. Susan Smith had just confessed to murdering her children. Now, she was trying to will away the whole nasty episode by saying, "I'm sorry."

In many ways, she was still such a child.

"Don't talk to nobody, don't radio, just go."

The divers got the urgent call from Sheriff Wells on Thursday afternoon. Their assignment was to return to a spot they'd already searched twice before—John D. Long Lake.

This time, however, when Wells and SLED Chief Robert Stewart met the team at the shoreline, they provided the men with precise instructions on where to look. Susan had watched her car float away with her children inside, still alive. She told them how far into the water it traveled before sinking.

Sergeant Francis Mitchum, the veteran diver, got the call at his home near Charleston, and was flown to Union by helicopter. He was joined by Steve Marr, the father who had volunteered for this detail. Steve Morrow, also a father, was there, too. Curtis Jackson was the first man to delve into the sixty-eight-degree water.

Last time, the divers went out thirty feet into the lake, at most. Now, Jackson ventured a full one hundred feet along the calm surface on this warm and windless afternoon, before plunging to a depth of eighteen feet.

At 4:15 P.M., just a few minutes after he left the shore, Jackson found a car. It was the Mazda. The vehicle had settled into a crevice in the lake's bottom that had previously eluded them. "As it turns out, another twenty minutes and they would have found it," said Greg Lucas, spokesman for the South Carolina Department of Natural Resources.

Mitchum and Marr grabbed lighting equipment and joined Jackson in the lake. The Mazda was upside-down, its doors and windows sealed shut. Shining the light into the car's windows, the men looked inside.

"They were pretty children," Mitchum managed to say. "But you couldn't have recognized them." The bodies, submerged for nine days, were waterlogged and swollen.

The men had been aware of what they were looking for, but it didn't help. Even with their combined decades of experience, they emerged from the water shaking.

Standing on the shore, the divers' tears mingled with the cold water dripping off their wet suits. They'd wanted badly to find the car, but prayed there would be no one inside.

"We hunt bodies all the time," said Mitchum, "but we don't find little children very often."

At home that night, Steve Morrow went directly into the room of his young son, and hugged him tightly. "I just needed to feel close to him," he said.

As the car was pulled out of the lake on chains, Sheriff Wells had no time to spare. He was in a hurry to see some friends.

The sheriff boarded a helicopter for the short hop to Mt. Vernon Estates, and landed on the vast, tree-exempt lawn near the Russell house. Wells was determined to beat the media to the home of Linda and Beverly Russell. It was the least he could do.

He was too late.

Some forty friends and family members gathered

around David Smith. Local television programs had been interrupted with unconfirmed reports of Susan's confession. A few in the house wept openly. Others, like Susan's brother Scotty Vaughan, Wells's dear friend, were determined not to believe the report until they heard it from the sheriff's mouth. But as soon as he walked into the door, Wells's expression told them everything.

David stared ahead, uncomprehending. He simply had never considered that Susan might have lied. Just that morning, he'd held her hand on the *Today* show, and announced to the world, "I'm behind her, 100 percent."

How could she do it?

The phone rang. It was David's mother, Barbara Benson, calling to tell her son to flip on the TV. Barbara had left Union a day earlier and was at her home near the South Carolina coast when a reporter called to inform her about the car and lake. At that point, all Barbara had heard was that her grandchildren's bodies had been found.

David's voice jerked so badly as he took the phone, his mother didn't recognize him. His entire being convulsed with violent sobs.

"David?" she asked. "David? David?"

"Sheriff Wells just confirmed it," he blurted out. "Susan confessed she killed the children."

"I'm sorry, I'm so sorry," his mother said. "I love you."

Then, she gave him the only words of comfort she could muster.

"Remember the Resurrection." David would see his boys again one day, his mother promised, in heaven.

"I know, Mom," David said, before hanging up.

David would not be comforted, though, not

now. Once off the phone, he locked himself in a bedroom. His father knocked on the door, but David
wouldn't let him in. He stayed in that bedroom for a
long time.

Later that night, David returned to his little
bachelor's apartment, a bare set of rooms whose
sole decorations were dozens of framed photographs of the children he would never hold again.
His mother drove in to Union late that night, tears
in her eyes. It was David who wound up making his
mom feel better. He was strong, calm—an attitude
his mother found more disturbing than David's crying bout.

David was in a state of shock and denial. He simply could not fathom how a woman he loved—still
loved—could do such a terrible thing. Maybe he
never would.

"Like I told them this morning, Mom," David
said, "I was behind her, 100 percent."

David said he wanted to talk to Susan, but his
family discouraged it. There were so many things he
wanted to ask her. David was convinced Susan
couldn't possibly have been in her right mind to kill
Michael and Alex. How else could this have happened? He needed to know.

Of all the people who should wish Susan ill,
David Smith was already searching for reasons to forgive her.

By Thursday afternoon, nine days had passed without
a break in the case, and many news correspondents
had already cleared out for the weekend. The
announcement that Wells would soon hold a press
conference sent many of them scrambling back to
Union.

It was dark by the time Wells stepped out into the parking lot outside the Union courthouse at 6:45, accompanied by SLED Chief Robert Stewart. By way of introduction, Wells warned the crowd of 300 reporters and spectators that he would answer no questions after delivering his statement.

"The vehicle, a 1990 Mazda driven by Smith, was located late Thursday afternoon in Lake John D. Long near Union," Wells said. "Two bodies were found in the vehicle's back seat.

"Mrs. Smith has been arrested, and will be charged with two counts of murder."

The gasp that burst spontaneously from the crowd was so loud, Stewart was startled. It was a sound, Stewart said, he would never forget.

But if Wells even heard the reaction, he didn't pause for a moment. He turned on his heel and walked off. The last nine days had been grueling. Now, the trauma was about to set in.

"Murderer!"

Just that morning, they gathered at the courthouse in Union to cry with her. Now, Union railed with fury as Sheriff Wells led Susan Smith into court to be booked on charges of double murder.

For more than a week, they'd searched the woods in cars and on foot, lit candles at the lake, and plastered leaflets everywhere in sight. For nine days, they'd prayed for the mother and her boys, put up their own money for a reward, and stood behind Susan when doubts were cast her way. All this time, they now realized, Susan Smith was toying with their emotions and messing with their minds.

"Baby killer!"

They gathered around Susan as a mob as she

walked into the courthouse, and hurled epithets at the woman's ponytailed head.

For many people, though, the enormity of her betrayal was too much to absorb all at once.

"This is not the same young woman I knew in high school," said Lewis Jeter III, a teacher who supervised Susan in the Junior Civitan Club, which helped disabled kids.

"If you could see the way she acted that night, that's the main thing that gets me," said Rick McCloud Jr., who made the 911 call after Susan knocked on his family's door the night of October 25, screaming about a carjacker.

"Just to think, for a solid week I was defending her. It gets me sick to my stomach."

Just like David, the people of Union were suspended in a state of shock and denial. They, too, had fallen in love with Susan. Here was a woman who never so much as screamed at her kids, and certainly never struck them. Susan, a murderer? She was so *nice.*

It would take time for the news to sink in to Susan's neighbor and booster, Alice Valentine. "I always believed her."

"I just couldn't imagine that Susan would do that," said Susan's grandmother, Sara Singleton, who lives near Los Angeles. "She always seemed to be such a devoted mother."

At Union's Winn-Dixie, Linda Fleming said, "I never in a million years would have thought that she could do something like this. She was always very nice.

"She was always smiling. I never heard her yell. She never hit them."

It was still too early to assess the extent of the damage Susan had inflicted. Members of the town's black community felt particularly injured. For nine days, every man aged seventeen to fifty felt as if he was under suspicion .

"This was a bad week to be a black man in Union," one man said.

"Black men don't steal babies. Black men don't kill babies," argued Howard Free, a black man who owns a shoe shop across from Union's courthouse. For days, that's exactly what Susan led so many to believe.

Other wounds showed up in the faces of small children, who watched the events unfold on TV.

"You wouldn't do me like that, would you, Mama?" a young boy asked his mother, who held him by the hand outside the courthouse.

"No, baby. Hush," his mother replied, and pulled him close to her breast.

The terrible question would be heard, time and time again, out of the mouths of babes. Susan Smith managed to do worse than kill. She tampered with the sacred bond between parent and child. As she walked into court, her very existence posed a grievous insult to mothers, and a mortal threat to their kids.

Over many nights to come, the people of Union would be haunted by the faces of Michael and Alex at the moment of death—panicked, helpless, screaming for their mother, as the Mazda turned into a watery coffin. There was no shutting out this vision; it grew only more horrible as the nights grew longer. As time went on, these thoughts would turn to fuel for their growing hatred.

But on Thursday night, Susan's crime was beyond comprehension. Why the heck didn't she just give them away?

Still another thing troubled the citizens of Union: How could the authorities allow Susan Smith to carry on for so long? Certainly they knew she was lying. Couldn't they have ended her charade sooner?

There was plenty of blame to go around.

Wells recovered sufficiently Thursday night to appear on the ABC news program *20/20*. The sheriff knew he had some explaining to do. He figured he'd start with Barbara Walters.

Barbara Walters: First, the tragedy that everyone is talking about. Yesterday morning, she was the heartbroken mother praying for the return of her two little boys. Today, Susan Smith was brought to court, charged with the murder of her children. The man you see escorting Mrs. Smith is the sheriff of Union County, South Carolina, and he joins us now for his first interview since Mrs. Smith's arrest.

Walters began by establishing that Susan was a friend and neighbor of the sheriff's, and that Susan's father committed suicide when she was a child. The sheriff was a bit stiff at the onset. As a lawman he was uncomfortable about giving away too much evidence before trial. But Wells needed to start telling the public why it took him so long to capture this criminal.

Strangely, he also displayed a need to protect Susan. Nine days spent locked together in a room apparently had unexpected side effects.

Walters: So she has a troubled background?

Howard Wells: I would say so, yes.

Walters: It is correct, Sheriff, that the two boys were alive when the car plunged into the water, and they drowned in the water?

Wells: That is our information, that's correct.

Walters: And did Mrs. Smith just jump out of the car before it went into the lake?

Wells: I cannot elaborate on any of the details of how it was accomplished.

On other matters, Wells was more forthcoming.

Walters: Were you surprised when Mrs. Smith confessed? You who have known her for so many years?

Wells: Yes, I knew something was wrong with the case, but I didn't know exactly her level of involvement.

Walters: You were with her today. We saw you in the pictures with her. What is her mood?

Wells: Well, she seems very heartbroken today, and she told me several times that she was very sorry, and that was the mood she seemed to portray to me.

Walters: Sorry that she had obviously done this to the children?

Wells: That's correct. . . . The only thing she asked me to communicate to her family was that she was sorry and that she still loved them all, and she hoped they still loved her.

Walters: Is there any bitterness because Susan Smith originally said that it was an African-American who had kidnapped the children?

Wells: During the investigation, we had to take the information as it was given to us, and she did identify the suspect as a black male, but during our investigation, we played that down to where we always said "abductor" or "suspect," except in the flyers that went out.

Walters: The whole country has been praying for these children, and for your town, which seemed like a wonderful little town, and now this horror. What do you say to your own people, what do you say to the rest of the country?

Wells: Well, we need a time for healing. Union County rose to the occasion, and everyone united and they stood together, and they prayed for this family and they prayed for the return of these two children. And I think we need to continue to pray for these two children, and pray for this mother and this family. Because of their loss, it's still just the same. And we will work through our problems here and I hope that the eyes of the world don't look at this negative and forget all the positives.

That night, Michael and Alex were home at last. They did not rest in their warm beds in the snug little house on Toney Road, but under the bright lights of a cold autopsy table. On the same night, their mother was transported out of the only town she had ever lived in, away from family members she'd seen every day of her life, to a detention facility in the neighboring county of York. There, her clothes were taken, and she was watched every second. Susan was never truly suicidal; jail guards made sure this was not about to change. From this time forward, Susan Smith would never be alone, but she was the loneliest woman in the world.

Early the next morning, she was due back in a town that no longer knew her. She was still Susan Smith. She just wasn't the woman they thought they knew.

She never really was.

11

Facing the Music

The problem is, we've been telling women for the last twenty years that abortion is okay. But why is it okay to kill a baby in the womb, but not after it's born? That's confusing. Maybe Susan Smith just didn't know where the line is drawn.

—Caller to a South Carolina radio talk show,
November 4, 1994.

My beeper went off during dinner in a Manhattan restaurant Thursday night. The urgent call was from Stuart Marques, metropolitan editor for my employer, the *New York Post.*

"Get on a plane," he said. When you're in the newspaper business, you get used to abrupt conversations and half-eaten meals.

Early the next morning, photographer David Rentas and I boarded the first USAir flight out of

LaGuardia en route to the Greenville-Spartanburg regional airport. During the nearly six years I'd worked for the *Post*, David and I have covered numerous assignments together in hot spots from Brooklyn to Somalia. In this case, the incredible impact Susan Smith's confession had made on the national psyche was evident from the instant I told the cabby my destination.

"You're going down there for that mother, aren't you?" he asked. "I got two kids. How could she do that? They should fry her."

It would only get worse.

Though we're both New York natives, David and I each have done tours of duty down South—David was a Marine stationed in South Carolina; I got my feet wet as a young reporter in places like West Virginia and Florida. Working in Florida for the *Tampa Tribune,* I was for a time assigned to bureaus in towns very much like Union: sparsely populated, Bible Belt outposts, where everyone knows each other and friendliness counts. But beneath the overt hospitality, David and I agreed, rural Southerners tend to be clannish to an extreme. Outsiders don't often manage to crack that carefully guarded facade.

When most Northerners consider South Carolina, they think of the elegant mansions of Charleston, the rowdy coastline of Myrtle Beach—attractive, vibrant tourist destinations that welcome strangers with open arms. Except for the common drawl, Union might as well be in another country.

Fiercely proud and pathologically polite, rural Southerners grapple daily with extraordinarily high rates of poverty and low rates of literacy, not to mention the insufferable arrogance of Northerners. More than a century after the Civil War, many denizens of Dixie still resent what they perceive as the carpetbagger mentality of the Yankee—that is, anyone who hails from a state north of Maryland. In reply, the rebel yell rings out loud and clear: Don't mess in our business.

To this day, North and South still glare at one other contemptuously across the Mason-Dixon line. You hear it in a New Yorker's tendency to dismiss South Carolinians as a bunch of hopeless rednecks. You see it in a white Southerner's stubborn refusal to discard his Confederate flags. Hang around South Carolina long enough, and you'll hear someone utter the slogan, "The South shall rise again." Although today, that old saying rolls off the tongue with an ironic laugh.

Some of the mistrust is simply due to personality. I'll never forget the pained expressions on the faces of burly Southern sheriffs when I first arrived in rural Florida as they encountered, for perhaps the first time, an aggressive, fast-talking lady reporter with a deadline. How does one act?

But friendships can blossom. It was out of mutual respect and curiosity that I became close to my bureau-mate, a North Carolinian, at the *Tribune*'s remote Crystal River bureau in 1984. One day, we were arguing ferociously about something I'm sure was terribly important—such as the culinary merits of North Carolina barbecue—when my pal stopped dead, her lilting drawl turned to ice, and she spat out the worst curse she could think of:

"Yankees!"

Ouch. I was blindsided by a stereotype. They cut both ways. Dumb hicks. Pushy New Yorkers. The Mason-Dixon is a fault line between two brash and exclusive worlds.

In truth, we have more in common, North and South, than many a hothead would care to notice. Everyone cares deeply about family, taxes, and crime.

We love our children equally. And thanks to that great cultural leveler—television—the whole nation for a short while found common ground behind Susan Smith. But on Friday, November 5, 1994, the gap between the two societies was about to widen into a gaping maw, as the army of Northern media types invaded Union.

It was with this in mind that we landed in Greenville, a nondescript-looking, landlocked Southern city containing a few office buildings, batches of residential subdivisions, and many, many strip shopping centers and fast-food chains. Greenville is comparable to a town on the edge of the frontier; Union is located, quite literally, in the middle of nowhere.

It wasn't long after David steered the rental car off Interstate 85 and headed southeast on Highway 176 that all evidence of civilization vanished. Ten miles outside of Greenville's neighboring city of Spartanburg, trees—tinged with November hues of red, yellow, and orange—dominate the landscape. For another twenty miles, the sea of timber sprawled before us, virtually unbroken by anything created by man.

The first sign of town appeared in the form of a yellow ribbon, affixed to a sign in front of a convenience store.

"We're praying for Michael and Alex," the sign read.

Soon, houses appeared, each one decked out in ribbons. By now, most of the yellow ones had already been replaced by sashes of black or blue, symbols of mourning for two little boys.

Finally, when we saw the golden arches of McDonald's, we knew we'd arrived.

By Friday, some of the press was camped out in Union's two noisy, low-rent motels, the Palmetto

Inn—instantly dubbed the "Palmetto Bug," a polite euphemism for the breed of giant, flying cockroach peculiar to the South—and the equally grungy American Economy Inn. Others chose to stay in Spartanburg, another unexceptional city that looks sophisticated in comparison to Union. Each morning, we'd brave that thirty-mile trek through the wilderness to arrive bright and early at the courthouse steps.

Friday morning was cranking up as another scorcher. By 9 A.M., the sun already beat down mercilessly on the shiny dome on top of the Union County courthouse. Sitting high atop a hill on Main Street, the courthouse is an imposing structure, fronted by fat, white columns that give Union the picture-postcard look of a genteel Southern town. On this day, even Union's grandest building was draped with huge yellow ribbons.

Scheduled for 10 was Susan Smith's bond hearing; it was her chance to ask a judge to set her free on bail. From early morning, correspondents from as far off as London lined up on the courthouse steps, vying for seats inside. Satellite trucks were stacked, two-deep, in front of the white columns. On the street, a crowd of onlookers—mothers carrying small babies, working stiffs who'd finagled a morning off—snaked around the building. Traffic along Union's ordinarily sleepy Main Street was hopelessly gridlocked as the entire planet, it seemed, rolled into town.

We all came hoping to catch a glimpse of Union's newest and most famous attraction: Susan Smith. If this event were in Los Angeles or New York, some clever entrepreneur would have roamed the sidewalk hawking soft drinks and T-shirts. Here, nobody looked like he was enjoying himself.

"Why don't y'all go home?" one woman said to reporters, hostility dripping from her drawl. To some people in town, the media invaders had already over-stayed their welcome.

On the roof of the courthouse, armed law-enforcement officials scanned the crowd for signs of trouble. Inside, SWAT team members, clad in gray bulletproof vests, fanned out in the courtroom where Susan was scheduled to appear.

Finally, as 10 A.M. drew near, the car carrying Susan approached the courthouse parking lot. The moment the newly dubbed "Monster Mother" emerged from the car with Sheriff Wells, the crowd stampeded.

"Baby-killing bitch!" a woman carrying her young daughter shouted at the top of her lungs.

"You murderer!"

Fists in the air, mouths twisted with rage, the crowd who came to denounce Susan Smith quickly transformed into a lynch mob. Cops formed a ring around the captive, keeping would-be gate crashers at bay. Nobody was going to hurt Susan Smith today.

Neither were the people going to get the show to which they felt entitled, after all Susan put them through. Sheriff Wells put one arm around his pris-oner protectively, and ushered her through a side door. With his free hand, the sheriff placed his coat over Susan's face, making sure that the only thing anyone saw of her was a ponytail, secured high on top of her head with a child's white bow.

Staked out at a spot inside the building, however, a photographer from the nearby Rock Hill *Herald,* scored the shot of a lifetime. The picture, beamed worldwide, showed Susan's bespectacled face pho-tographed through a windowpane, her slender wrists sealed together by a pair of thick steel handcuffs. She looks like she's praying.

The line of spectators crawled into the courthouse like fans at a high-security rock concert, as scores of reporters, curiosity-seekers, and family members had their bags searched and their bodies patted down by sheriff's deputies. Finally, everybody took seats on dark, wooden pews in the sun-drenched courtroom, waiting to see Susan face the music. Upstairs, in a balcony where blacks were restricted not so long ago, TV cameras prepared to record her every move.

But the show for which many of us had traveled thousands of miles was canceled. Instead of Susan in chains, we had to make do with lawyers in suits.

The first to speak was David Bruck, a Harvard-educated attorney who specializes in keeping killers out of South Carolina's electric chair. He informed Judge Larry Patterson that Susan was giving up her right to be present at the hearing. She would not ask for bail, nor would she enter a plea. Instead, Susan Smith agreed to be locked up in the women's detention center near Columbia. Solicitor Tommy Pope, the six-foot-four prosecutor in charge of Union and York counties, had nothing to argue about this morning.

They were in and out of court in just a few minutes.

By the time Susan was led out the back door, the mob had grown both in numbers and intensity.

"Hold your head up! You're a baby murderer!" shrieked one woman.

"Give her to the people," suggested another. Susan was going to need all the security she could get.

As she drove off to jail, someone asked David Bruck about Susan's state of mind.

"She is heartbroken," said Bruck, forty-five.

Lean and soft-spoken with a generous head of salt-and-pepper hair, Bruck did his best to shine a sympathetic light on his client.

"She is mourning her children," he said.

But there was little fondness for Susan Smith on Main Street.

The crowd fanned out on the sidewalk, each lapel decorated with pictures of Michael and Alex. They wanted always to be reminded of those little faces.

Lisa White, twenty-four, a high-school classmate of Susan's, walked purposefully up and down the block in front of the courthouse, carrying her daughter, Brooke. Brooke, a little beauty with wide, blue eyes and corn-silk hair gathered in a tiny barrette, waved at strangers who stopped by to admire her, then buried her face demurely in her mother's hair. At fourteen months, Brooke was the same age as Alex when he died. Lisa wanted people to meet her, and to see what Susan stole from the world when she killed Alex.

"I want everyone to know my baby is precious to me," said Lisa. "I gave life to her. There's no way I would take it from her. Life is too short already."

Lisa was torn by conflicting emotions—she and Susan had been in Union High's Beta Club, the organization for gifted students, and socialized together after graduation. Just a month earlier, Lisa and Susan attended a birthday party for Susan's friend, Tracy Lovelace. Michael and Alex didn't come, but Susan always seemed eager to be around children.

"Susan got my baby and walked to the park with her," said Lisa. "She seemed happy. She just seemed like nothing was wrong."

Like so many in Union, Lisa believed Susan throughout the ordeal of the last nine days. She drove out to Monarch to search for the boys, and passed out flyers all over town.

"This is like a dream, and I haven't woken up yet. She was my friend. But I have no sympathy for her."

"Justice will be done," the young mother said with finality. "Her day will come."

Across the street, April Vinson, another of Susan's high-school chums, stood with her three-week-old daughter, Kayla, snuggled against her chest.

"She was a nice girl," April said of Susan. "She never did no harm to anybody. She was sweet to everybody and smart as a whip."

But then, April started talking about Susan's overdoses. Her father's suicide. The ugly scenes between Susan and David at Winn-Dixie, where April worked before having her baby. They were clues to what happened, but not excuses.

"She showed good love and affection to those kids," said April. "She loved them with all her heart." April paused. The murders, she was certain, were not the unintentional act of a deranged creature, but the calculated work of a woman who wanted her kids out of her life.

"Deep down in her heart, she knew she killed her kids. How in the world can a mother do that?"

Others were not so introspective. Besides Susan Smith, the murder case against O.J. Simpson and the coming election were hot topics of conversation in Union. Crime and punishment were on a lot of people's minds.

"The electric chair is too good for her," said one man. "They should do to her what she done to those kids."

On talk radio, that barometer of populist sensibility, callers wanted to discuss nothing but the killer mother. Several expressed outrage over the cavalier manner in which Susan Smith blamed her crime on a phantom black carjacker. And they were incensed that the investigation took so long to conclude.

"This is just another example of African-Americans being demonized and blamed for all of society's ills," one caller complained.

One woman caller irritated the radio host by suggesting that Susan may have been led astray by the ready availability of legal abortions:

"The problem is, we've been telling women for the last twenty years that abortion is okay. But why is it okay to kill a baby in the womb, but not after it's born? That's confusing. Maybe Susan Smith just didn't know where the line is drawn."

Most callers, though, were not ready to accept any excuse for child murder, regardless of their social views. Many were livid about the so-called abuse-excuses used to defend the perpetrators of violent crimes, from Lorena Bobbitt's penis-slicing in Virginia, to the Menendez brothers' killing of their parents in California. The people of South Carolina were adamant that Susan Smith take responsibility for her own hideous acts.

"They should string her up on Main Street," one man exclaimed on the air. "Make an example of her."

The attacks on Susan grew ever fiercer as people contemplated the utter senselessness of the murders.

"If she didn't want those boys, she should have left them on the courthouse steps," one black woman said on Main Street. "Someone would have taken them in a minute."

And the crying didn't stop at Union's city limits.

In New York, Kathie Lee Gifford, who has used her nationally televised *Regis and Kathie Lee* morning talk show to make the name of her son, Cody, a household word, told her co-host, Regis Philbin, that she cried her eyes out when she learned Michael and Alex Smith were found dead in the lake.

In Duluth, Minnesota, President Bill Clinton,

campaigning on behalf of Democratic candidates, steered his comments away from the coming election to say his "thoughts and prayers" were with the people of Union.

"Like every American, and especially every parent, I have followed this gripping incident and it has been a heartbreaking thing," the president said.

Clinton placed two personal calls to Sheriff Wells, his fellow Democrat, to praise him for police work that led to the arrest of Susan Smith. He also thanked Wells for using restraint and good judgment in handling the investigation, and preventing the case from triggering racial unrest. Wells shrugged when asked to describe the contents of the conversations; the president, battling for the future of his party, didn't really have much to say.

The comments that drew the biggest gasp, however, came out of the mouth of Newt Gingrich, the Republican congressman from Georgia and, at the time, the House minority whip. In a tape-recorded interview with an Associated Press reporter in Atlanta, Gingrich used the Union child slayings to make a point about Americans' concerns regarding crime and the Democratic leadership as Election Day approached. He said:

"How a mother can kill her two children, fourteen months and three years, in the hopes that her boyfriend would like her is just a sign of how sick the system is and I think people want to change. The only way you get change is to vote Republican. That's the message for the last three years."

Gingrich was roundly criticized for milking the tragedy for political ends, and he later protested that his remarks were taken out of context. The controversy didn't stop Republican candidates from steamrolling through the election November 8, winning a majority of seats in both the House and Senate. Gingrich was quickly elevated to the position of Speaker of the House.

Amid the din of anger and recrimination, the saddest words of all were said on Toney Road. With tears in her eyes, Alice Valentine, Susan Smith's longtime neighbor and supporter, looked over at the lawn where she'd watched little Michael and Alex play.

"I'm just stunned and disappointed in the mother," she said. "Evidently they were in the way."

She then dared utter aloud what everyone in town was thinking. "I just hope they were asleep or something and didn't know the horror of dying alone in that car."

But it was not to be. On Friday, authorities summarized the preliminary findings of the autopsies performed on the Smith boys: Michael and Alex were very much alive when their mother drowned them in the lake.

What's more, the sealed Mazda had floated, possibly for a long time, before it filled, slowly, with cold water. One law-enforcement source estimated it may have taken as long as forty minutes for the sealed car to travel 100 feet, roll over, and sink eighteen feet to the bottom.

No one could have slept through that.

David Smith remained secluded in his apartment. But he, too, could not avoid news of his sons' gruesome fate. In the hours since Susan confessed to murder, David was surrounded by his parents, his stepmother, and friends. He cried intermittently, then stared at the photographs of his boys as if in a stupor.

"Why? Why? Why?" David asked over and over.

Susan Smith before the murders.

(Photo credit: © *A Current Affair* / SYGMA)

Susan and baby Michael. Susan wrote
in her diary that she had given birth to "the most
beautiful baby boy in the world."

(Photo credit: © *A Current Affair* / SYGMA)

Michael and Alex Smith.

(Photo credit: American Fast Photo / SYGMA)

Susan Smith after her confession and arrest.

(Photo credit: Andy Burriss, The Rock Hill *Herald* / SYGMA)

The crowd came to Union County courthouse
for Susan Smith's arraignment.

(Photo credit: David Rentas, *New York Post*)

Talk show host Oprah Winfrey was one of the many
who came to the lake where the Smith boys drowned.

(Photo credit: David Rentas, *New York Post*)

Pallbearers carry the single white casket bearing the
bodies of Michael and Alex Smith.

(Photo credit: David Rentas, *New York Post*)

David Smith is
overcome with
grief at the
funeral of his
sons.

(Photo credit:
David Rentas,
New York Post)

Susan Leigh Vaughan was voted the "friendliest"
girl of the Union High School class of 1989.

(Photo credit: David Rentas, *New York Post*)

"Why didn't she just return them to me? I would have taken them. I'd even pay the child support," David pleaded with his father, as if the offer somehow could bring the boys back.

There was much talk of the hereafter, and of the Resurrection. It did little to soothe the grieving father.

"If I live on sixty more years," David said, "will I have to live that long to see my kids?"

But it was his eerie bouts of calm that proved the most troubling to the people closest to David. They worried that he was locked in a state of shock.

One close friend, W. T. Williford, twenty, the dairy manager at Winn-Dixie, went over to David's apartment to comfort his pal, only to find that "he was calming me down. I was the one who was crazy."

"He's hurtin'," W. T. surmised. "But he's trying to hold it in. He don't understand it, neither. He don't even know what's going on.

"He loves his kids. She loved 'em, too."

As W. T. spoke outside the supermarket, his mother, Janie, smoked a cigarette, her eyes red-rimmed and swollen. "You never seen her without those kids," she said.

That night, David's and Susan's families faced a difficult task. Together, they had to plan a funeral.

The Russells and the Smiths, joined by their children's marriage, always enjoyed cordial relations. But on Friday night, the couple who'd just learned their grandchildren were murdered sat down with the couple whose daughter confessed to the killings. The awkwardness of the situation was tempered by the fact that Susan's parents had lost their grandchildren, too. They all decided that animosity was not only unnecessary, but un-Christian. They would see Michael and Alex off into the next world with all the love and dignity they deserved.

The funeral was scheduled for the following Sunday, at Buffalo United Methodist Church, the house of worship that Susan and David attended most Sundays. Then the children would be buried at the small country cemetery adjacent to Bogansville United Methodist Church, where David and Susan were married. David wanted his boys to find eternal rest next to his dear brother, Daniel. To achieve that end, Daniel's grave had to be moved a few feet to an empty spot, with room enough beside it for his nephews.

David had one last, pressing request. He wanted Michael and Alex to be buried in the same coffin.

"They would have wanted that," David told his family.

Michael and Alex would spend the rest of eternity as they spent their short lives, secure in each other's company.

Meanwhile, a minor player in the case who made a huge splash in the headlines was busy packing his bags. Tom Findlay, the wealthy "Catch" who, by dumping Susan, may have unwittingly driven her to murdering her sons, received a number of death threats. Through his lawyer at Conso, he issued a statement to the *Union Daily Times* newspaper. His words were chosen far more carefully than those in the computer-generated "Dear John" letter that Tom sent to Susan a little more than two weeks earlier.

"I am devastated by this tragedy," Tom's statement began.

"I cooperated with and have been cooperating with legal authorities since last week in the disappearance of Susan Smith's children. The only reason I am coming forward to issue this statement now is because of the continuing inaccurate reports of my relationship with Susan Smith.

"I did have a relationship with Ms. Smith and on October the 18th I told her that I was terminating that relationship for a number of reasons and gave her a copy of a letter to that effect—a letter which I gave to the authorities early in this investigation. One of the reasons for my termination of the relationship was that I was not ready to assume the important responsibilities of being a father. However, that was far from the only reason for terminating the relationship and certainly was not the most important. At no time did I suggest to Ms. Smith that her children were the only obstacle in any potential relationship with her."

Tom wrote that he would continue cooperating with authorities, as needed, then closed his statement with:

"I share in the grief of this community in the loss of these two children."

Shortly afterward, Tom left town. Friends said he went to London where his father, J. Cary Findlay, the richest man in Union, was opening a new textile plant.

Nobody slept well Friday night. David Smith spent the night staring at his dead sons' pictures, long after his visitors ran out of words to say. The Russells opened their fine house to friends and relatives, who brought over so much food that was destined to spoil.

Reporters, touched in ways I have never seen before by the overwhelming grief engulfing Union, sat up and wondered how they'd make it through another day of this awful assignment.

Down in Columbia, Susan was alone locked into a cell measuring six-by-fourteen feet. It contained a sink and a toilet and a small window that looked out into a world she was no longer a part of.

Susan was on suicide watch. Her clothes were taken, and she was handed a paper gown to wear, out of fear that she might try to fashion fabric into a noose. Every fifteen minutes, a guard checked on her through a second window facing into the prison, then recorded her every movement in a log.

Susan was allowed to wear her glasses and was provided a blanket. That was about it, as far as amenities were concerned. However, the girl who gave up everything to live in a castle was given one, solitary possession—a Bible. Through the long, sleepless night, she cradled the black-covered volume, reading from the book of Psalms out loud. The Bible was Susan's only friend in her tiny, new world.

12
How Long?

Those babies had to have suffered.

—Scuba diver Francis Mitchum, after locating the
bodies of Michael and Alex Smith at the bottom of
John D. Long Lake.

How many minutes ticked by from the instant Susan Smith's burgundy Mazda touched the water of John D. Long Lake until the moment it settled on the muddy bottom?

How long did little Michael and Alex Smith, strapped helplessly in the car's back seat, suffer in the chilly, catfish-stocked water before death overtook them?

And after Susan Smith sent her children splashing into the lethal lake—with their mother screaming, "Oh God! Oh God, no! What have I done?"—did she have sufficient time to go back and save them? Or else, did she have time to call someone to help to pull the boys out alive? Time she then frittered away by spinning a web of lies intended to save her own skin?

How long did Michael and Alex live in that car, terrified, screaming, gasping for air? The precise number of heartbeats may be impossible to gauge. But experts speculate it could have been as little as five to ten minutes.

Or as long as forty.

The question of how long the children suffered not only preys on the mind, it forms a pertinent piece of evidence in the case against Susan Smith. The level of pain inflicted on crime victims is a matter judges and juries take seriously. And that is why the calculations of forensic experts are potentially damaging—not to mention heart-breaking.

They could show that the blood coursing through Susan Smith's veins runs colder than the water of John D. Long Lake.

Think about it. Look at a clock, and try holding your breath for five minutes. You can't do it. Now, imagine someone is holding your face in a tub of water for the same amount of time. Panic would engulf your entire being within seconds.

However long it took Michael and Alex to die, the physical evidence indicates that the end did not come quickly.

For one thing, the car floated into the lake for a long distance. During the nine days that Susan's Mazda was the most sought-after car in America, the sedan was sitting just beyond investigators' noses. Twice, experienced frogmen spent hours looking near the shoreline of John D. Long Lake. Twice, they came up empty-handed.

But on November 3, after Susan Smith pinpointed to authorities the spot where she dumped her car and its precious cargo, and described how the Mazda floated off, divers were able to locate the vehicle within minutes. Incredibly, they found that the car had skimmed along the lake's surface for 100 feet—much farther than the experts had expected—before it toppled on its back and slowly sank into a deep crevice eighteen feet below.

How could an automobile weighing well over a ton respond like that? And what does that suggest about the boys trapped inside?

In an attempt to answer some of these questions, a forensics team went over the Mazda with a fine-tooth comb. Armed with revised information about the condition of the car, the experts were able to make far more precise calculations about its potential behavior than they had before the vehicle was found.

As it turned out, the car, though constructed of sturdy steel, behaved like a toy balloon.

First of all, the Mazda's windows were rolled up on the night Susan took it for its final spin. When the car hit the water, the sealed-off interior formed an air pocket that made it float.

Perhaps even more significantly, the car's gas tank was nearly empty when the divers found it. Apparently, on the night of October 25, as Susan circled for three hours around Union County on her harrowing journey down memory lane, she never bothered to stop for fuel.

With the Mazda about out of gas, John D. Long Lake represented the end of the road for this family, in more ways than one. Susan may not have realized it at the time, but the virtually empty gas tank created a natural flotation device that might have contributed to prolonging her children's lives.

As the steel balloon moved out into the lake, the laws of physics that made the car float soon conspired to sink it. Though the car is reasonably airtight, tiny fissures allow water to enter, in this case slowly, into the vehicle. Traveling on water, a car has no traction, so its speed would be difficult to determine. But what is known is that the Mazda moved out fully 100 feet before the water inside grew heavy enough to topple the car. That the Mazda was found lying upside-down indicates that the sixty-eight-degree water filled up the space above the boys' heads first. As the water seeped in, gradually it reached the faces of Michael and Alex.

As heavier water continued to displace the air, the Mazda was pulled downward, ever downward, to its final resting place.

All of which leads to the question: Could she have saved them?

The distance from the shore of John D. Long Lake to the home of Rick and Shirley McCloud measures approximately 1,500 feet. Traveling on foot, the first part of that journey involves walking up a gently sloping path. Then, it's a short stroll along the flat pavement of Highway 49 before the pedestrian arrives at the McClouds' lighted front porch.

On the night of October 25, the moon was two-thirds full. Walking—not running, not meandering—from the shoreline, up the moonlit path, across the highway to the McClouds' front door should take the average person about eight or nine minutes to accomplish. On the night she showed up at the McClouds' place, Susan was so hysterical and out of breath, the family assumed she had been running.

Eight or nine minutes, at a normal walking rate. Could she have saved her children? In her handwritten confession, Susan suggested otherwise.

"I wanted to turn around so bad and go back," she wrote, "but I knew it was too late."

What if Susan had run up that path? Could this story have had a happier ending?

Whether Susan, who lied to the entire world for nine days about her crime, was sincere when she claimed that her deadly decision was irreversible is something known only by her. As to whether there was enough time for Susan to call someone to help rescue the boys—the final word on that mystery may have died at the bottom of the lake. The best guesses of the experts will have to serve as a reasonable substitute on dry land.

But what troubled investigators and Union residents alike was the fact that Susan Smith never, for one instant, tried to save them.

For that alone, they will never forgive her.

13
Mothers Who Kill

I know indeed what evil I intend to do,
but stronger than all my afterthoughts is my fury,
fury that brings upon mortals the greatest evils.

—Euripides' *Medea*, 431 B.C.

The act strikes us as unnatural. Mother—the giver of life—murders the child she carried inside her, fed and nurtured. She snuffs the breath from a helpless being who depends upon her for his every need. So alien is the crime to our way of thinking, we try to deny it even exists.

Not everyone has children, but we've all had mothers. So perhaps because of the threat such an act poses to our own security, we feel obligated to fall for every tear-drenched entreaty from a mom who claims her kid was snatched from a shopping mall the moment she turned her back. We give the benefit of the doubt to each distraught young woman who cries that she "dropped" her bruised and battered baby.

And when the truth emerges—she strangled her infant, she broke his neck—we turn to a ready list of excuses that satisfy our need to believe the heinous crime was an aberration: The mother was suffering from postpartum depression. She was abused as a child. Her husband beat her. She was stressed-out; she snapped.

Western culture continues to romanticize motherhood, in spite of the wide number of family choices now available to women. Domestic violence is reserved for the occasional movie-of-the-week, while everyday films and situation comedies celebrate the career woman who jumps off the fast track in favor of fulfilling what we're told is everywoman's true nature: Maternity.

Dr. Lee Leifer, a psychiatrist who has treated many mothers who've killed, refers to this as the "American myth of what it takes to be a mother."

"We assume women are born with love for children, when they are not," says Leifer, assistant professor of clinical psychiatry at Columbia University Medical School of Physicians and Surgeons in New York.

Killing one's baby, he says, "goes against the cultural norm—the need for men in our society to feel that women are care-giving and nurturing."

In reality, murderous acts committed by mothers, while uncommon, aren't nearly as rare as we'd like to believe. And that's been a fact of life since at least the beginning of recorded history.

More than 2,400 years ago, a writer of Greek tragedy gave us Medea, that classical precursor to Susan Smith. Enraged after being spurned by her lover, Medea killed the two sons she bore. Euripides didn't invent this character out of thin air. Medea certainly was not the first woman to go the baby-killing route; Susan Smith is not the last.

Nor is covering up the evidence with a tall tale a unique phenomenon. Just three days before Susan Smith reported hysterically that her sons were stolen, a strikingly similar child-snatching drama was playing out near Fort Lauderdale, Florida. Pauline Zile, twenty-four, told police that she was shopping with her seven-year-old daughter, Christina Holt, at the Swap Shop flea market west of the beach front community when her little girl disappeared from a stall in the women's rest room.

It was daytime, but there were no witnesses. Police had not one clue as to what happened to the child. For five days, Pauline pleaded tearfully on television, begging anyone in earshot to provide information that might help find Christina. As Pauline spoke to reporters, she ran her fingers tenderly through the hair of a doll she described as her daughter's favorite.

Police now believe the mother bought that doll to use as a TV prop.

On October 27, as the Susan Smith ordeal was cranking into high gear over in South Carolina, the gory truth emerged in Florida. From the start, police were troubled that Pauline referred to her little girl in the past tense the moment she was gone—"She *was* a nice girl." During a search of the mother's apartment, police found a bloody pair of jeans. Cornered, Pauline Zile dropped her kidnapping fable, and claimed her husband, John, had beaten the little girl to death.

John Zile led authorities to a five-foot-deep, hand-dug grave behind a nearby K-Mart discount store, where Christina was buried. The little girl was never at the Swap Shop.

According to police reports, six weeks earlier, John beat Christina savagely over the face and body as Pauline watched. John Zile later told cops that Pauline joined in the beating. When Christina started screaming, John shoved a towel into the little girl's mouth, and she choked and went into seizures. John tried performing cardiopulmonary resuscitation, but Christina died. For four days, the couple hid Christina's corpse in a closet, before they finally decided to bury her remains. John Zile was charged with the child's murder.

Pauline's attempt to throw the entire blame for Christina's death on her man didn't work. The announcement that Pauline Zile would also be charged with murder came just seventeen hours after Sheriff Howard Wells of Union announced that Susan Smith faced murder charges in South Carolina.

If two similar cases occurring virtually at the same time sounds like a bizarre coincidence, think again: During a three-month period before Christmas 1994, at least four children were slain by their mothers, fathers, or both in the state of Florida alone. One man stuffed his little girl under a waterbed mattress, alive. Whether motivated by greed, as suspected in the case of Susan Smith, or pure, blind rage, the result is the same: dead children. The only differences are the lengths to which the killers go to conceal their misdeeds.

If the public doesn't want to believe that parents kill children, authorities are forced to face the facts. Abductions by strangers, not mothers, are the aberration.

A prevailing myth that's taken hold of the American mind has earned the pithy label Stranger Danger. It suggests that the woods and shopping malls are jam-packed with perverts prepared to steal a child the second the mother turns away. Though the risk can't be ignored, the threat posed by strangers is minimal compared to the hype the phenomenon has received.

In truth, such instances are so isolated, we remember the victims' names for a long time: Polly Klaas of California, Sarah Ann Wood of upstate New York, Etan Patz of Manhattan. To this day, the Lindbergh baby's kidnapping of the 1930s remains a mystery to be reckoned with. All this illustrates the fact that no evidence exists whatsoever that an army of strange men lurks in the shadows, hunting for children to sell into slavery, to remove their organs for shipping to Mexico, or to sacrifice them in black-magic rituals—all stories that have fallen upon the ears of officials in the National Center for Missing and Exploited Children in Arlington, Virginia. A combination think tank and clearinghouse for cases of stolen and abused kids, the private, nonprofit center is funded by a Justice Department grant, and its staffers work closely with the Federal Bureau of Investigation.

Take a close look at the carton next time you drink milk. Chances are, the missing child pictured on the side is the victim of what's called "custodial interference." That is, one parent hides a kid from the other, either to protect her from abuse or simply out of spite. Not a healthy way for a child to grow up, experts contend. But not necessarily lethal, either.

The most comprehensive study on the matter was conducted by three researchers: Dr. David Finkelhor of the University of New Hampshire, Dr. Gerald Hotaling of Lowell University, and Dr. Andrea Sedlak of Westat, Inc. They found that the number of children abducted by family members nationwide in 1988 totaled some 354,100—far higher than earlier estimates of 25,000 to 100,000.

The most unexpected statistic to emerge from their work, however, was the smallest. The researchers pegged the number of children snatched by strangers each year at a mere 200 to 300.

That number is disputed by Ruben Rodriguez, the senior analyst for the Center for Missing and Exploited Children—but not by much. Rodriguez believes the 200-to-300 estimate ignores cases in which a kidnapper takes a child in order to commit a far more serious crime, such as rape. The rape, he believes, absorbs the attention of authorities, who then fail to classify the crime as a stranger abduction.

Even so, Rodriguez pegs the number of stranger abductions at 500 to 600 annually—still considerably lower than the thousands of children many people believe are stolen off the streets of America each year.

On one thing researchers are in unanimous agreement: The vast majority of murdered children under the age of five are killed by parents. The FBI estimated that 662 children aged four and younger were slain in 1992—more than two-thirds of them by one or both parents. But that number only tells a fraction of the story. Another 1,100 children died from abuse or neglect during the same year, according to U.S. Department of Health and Human Services statistics.

There are many who believe even that enhanced body count is low. Sometimes parents cover up murder by claiming a child died from Sudden Infant Death Syndrome, or accidents. Some researchers estimate that as many as half the parent-killers get away with murder.

Who's doing the killing?

Parents who kill span the spectrum of gender, race, and class. Rodriguez cites the case of a policeman in San Bernadino, California, who beat his two-year-old daughter to death because she violated household rules by raiding the refrigerator after permissible hours. After killing his daughter, the father told fellow police officers that the girl vanished in a shopping mall the moment he turned his back.

"Dad cuts up the body, burns it, places it in concrete which he dries into cinder blocks that he disposes of throughout the county in different areas," Rodriguez says. After he was found out, the murderous cop committed suicide.

"I use this case in my training course to show it cuts across all social classes, all ethnicities. It runs the gamut of race, religion, and type. This kind of crime is not specific to any type or kind of individual."

Nor is child-killing a regional phenomenon. Parents commit murder in small towns and villages, in rural areas and major cities at about the same rate.

More fathers kill than mothers, but that trend reverses when the dead child is very young. "Under five years of age, Mother has total control of the child," explains Rodriguez. "The child is not in school, and not under the care of anybody else."

But when the parent tries to cover her tracks, the lies that are told tend to follow predictable patterns.

"The two biggest scenarios used to cover up a death are what we call the 'mall scenario' and the 'pick-up scenario,'" Rodriguez says breezily.

The lingo of the murdered-children experts may sound flip to the uninitiated, but it's no different from the shorthand spoken by doctors and nurses, reporters and cops—anyone who faces horrible death every day on the job. Rodriguez sees so much of this kind of thing, he's developed a nose for sniffing out rotten abduction cases with minimal information.

The case of Pauline Zile, who allegedly helped

kill her child, then blamed it on a stranger in the Swap Shop, fits the "classic mall scenario," he says:

"She says, 'I was in the bathroom stall when the child was abducted.' That's often how these stories go."

Susan Smith's tale, on the other hand, fits into the category of pick-up story. "It might go, 'I ran into the 7-Eleven for just a second, and my child was taken out of the car.' However you want to color it, the mother says, 'The children were taken from me.' It's a version of the pick-up story."

In spring 1994, a French-Canadian couple found their ten-week-old daughter dead in her crib. Afraid of being accused of killing her, the parents dumped her body in the woods 100 miles from home. Then they drove their pickup truck over the border and stopped in New York City, where they told police the baby disappeared in Central Park. For two days, helicopters, bloodhounds, and scuba divers searched the park, until the couple broke down and told the truth. Apparently, they believed the world would buy the fallacy that children get swallowed up every day by New York.

Pick-up story or mall scenario, the yarns have one common giveaway: No witnesses.

"My first question to the FBI is, 'When were the children last seen alive by someone else other than the mother?'" Rodriguez says.

When confronted with a child's body, experts can predict with relative certainty whether the killer was male or female, based on such things as the placement of the corpse. Women tend to place the body within three miles of home. "She'll wrap it in a blanket and put it in a shallow grave close to her," says Rodriguez. Or, like Susan Smith, she'll drown the children close to where she lives.

Men, on the other hand, might travel up to 350 miles, and mutilate or dismember a body to obscure evidence of the crime.

In addition, women tend to concoct more elaborate stories to explain a child's disappearance.

Back in 1965, people throughout New York City were traumatized when Alice Crimmons, forever referred to as a divorced, red-haired cocktail waitress from Queens, claimed someone broke into the window of her ground-floor apartment and killed her four-year-old daughter and five-year-old son. But authorities decided that Alice wanted her children out of the way so that she could take off with her boyfriend, a wealthy contractor, and alleged Alice Crimmons masterminded the break-in herself.

Alice was found guilty in the strangulation deaths of her children, although a manslaughter conviction in her son's killing was overturned on appeal. In 1977, Alice was freed on parole. In the end, she sailed off into the sunset on the yacht of her boyfriend, who stood by her throughout the entire twelve-year episode.

In another case with striking similarities to Susan Smith's, Diane Downs of Eugene, Oregon, in 1983 reported that a "shaggy-haired stranger" tried to commandeer her car on a dark, deserted road. When she said no, Diane claimed, the villain shot her three sleeping children. The mother could provide no reasonable explanation why the man let her escape unscathed. Police, however, had a clue. Like Susan Smith, Diane Downs had a boyfriend who didn't want to have anything to do with raising kids.

Cheryl Downs, age seven, died from her wounds, while four-year-old Danny was paralyzed. Eight-year-old Christy suffered a stroke. But she lived to testify that her mother was the one who pulled the trigger.

Based on Christy's heart-wrenching testimony, Diane Downs was convicted in the slayings and sentenced to life in prison. She escaped briefly in 1987. When she was caught, Diane claimed she was out looking for her children's attacker.

The fact that women feel comfortable inventing fantastic stories may stem from the public's reverence for motherhood, combined with the widely held myth that a woman isn't capable of killing her own child.

"With both Susan Smith and Pauline Zile, who does the camera gravitate to?" Rodriguez poses. "To the mama. She's the one crying. Dad is to the right or to the left, giving moral support. The camera's on her; she gets the sympathy."

Meanwhile, John Zile was perceived by many as what Rodriguez calls a "dirtball."

"Can you see this man going on camera saying, 'Help us find our baby?' The community wouldn't gravitate to him, it would gravitate to the mother." David Smith, while no dirtball, played second-string to Susan as a media star.

The stories fall apart, however, because the killings and cover-ups tend not to be carefully premeditated. "You're looking at desperation. In a lot of these cases they don't plan the killing, and they have to do everything on the fly."

In the Susan Smith case, Rodriguez worked closely with the FBI, watching tapes of Susan's public statements. He immediately focused on two things: With each successive press conference, David graduated from standing next to Susan to holding her hand to putting his arm around her; she seemed to demand an ever-increasing level of support in order to continue spinning her story. Another telling tidbit was that Susan studiously avoided making eye contact with the TV cameras.

When the unthinkable comes true, and a mother is revealed to be the killer, the public's tendency to protect her doesn't erase automatically.

"If Mom does it, there's sympathy for the mother. There may be other dynamics here, like postpartum depression. Society says she must be under a lot of pressure.

"If the father victimizes the child, it's much more heinous. Society says, 'Here's a strong man beating this two-year-old child to death.'"

Susan Smith may be heckled in the street, but her attorney is well aware of the possibilities for exploiting the public's compassionate nature. Since Susan's arrest, David Bruck uses words like "fragile" to describe his client, who always appears in court with her hair in a frilly bow.

But are baby-killers worthy of our compassion? What is it that makes them kill?

Psychologists have more success explaining why women murder their husbands than they do determining why women strangle, smother, or shoot the kids.

The literature is filled with cases of mothers who apparently harm or kill children to draw attention to themselves. Marybeth Tinning of Schenectady, New York, had all nine of her children die inexplicably between 1972 and 1985. She was convicted of the final child's murder in 1986.

When all five of Waneta Hoyt's children died mysteriously between 1965 and 1971, she chalked up the deaths to Sudden Infant Death Syndrome—or SIDS. More than two decades later, a local prosecutor, suspicious of that explanation, interrogated the mother, who confessed she suffocated the children with pillows, a towel, or her shoulder. Though she later recanted the confession, Waneta Hoyt was charged with five counts of murder.

The common psychological explanation for this is "Munchausen's syndrome by proxy." With Munchausen's syndrome, adults pretend they're sick, or actually make themselves ill in order to win attention. The "by proxy" addition implies the adult makes a child sick—or kills him—in a bid for sympathy. Susan Smith's behavior after she drowned her sons suggests spotlight-grabbing was one of her motives.

But what makes a woman turn out this way? At the Behavioral Science Unit at FBI headquarters in Quantico—also known as the "Silence of the Lambs Unit"—agents study personal and environmental factors that create killers.

"Generally you're talking about a woman with low self-esteem, emotionally immature, she's socially immature," says Rodriguez. "She's young, financially strapped, emotionally strapped.

"We see a lot of cases, the Smith case is one example, where the child becomes a hindrance in a relationship. The man says, 'No, thank you, I don't want a ready-made family.'

"She says, 'I'm living alone, I have an adulterous husband, I'm involved in relationships, too,'—all these dynamics are present for this woman to make her decision."

In other ways, Susan does not fit the mold of the typical killer. Experts point to a woman's isolation—her lack of a safety net of friends and family—as contributing to a woman's desperation. "She says, 'I've had enough. The only solution I can come up with is, I must eliminate those children.'" But in the case of Susan Smith, friends and family were in ample supply; she had many places to turn for monetary and emotional support.

Spousal abuse can be a factor, too, in making women accept, or participate in, violence against children. In New York, Hedda Nussbaum was battered to a pulp for years by her lawyer-lover Joel Steinberg. She stood by, cowed and supportive, as Steinberg inflicted beatings that ultimately killed six-year-old Lisa, the couple's illegally adopted daughter.

But there was never as much as a hint that David hit Susan. Except for her unsubstantiated, and later recanted, claim of molestation by her stepfather, there is no evidence that Susan suffered abuse at the hands of any man.

Instead, Susan apparently was backed into a corner by the very loving network on which she depended. Their scrutiny prevented Susan from giving away her children to someone who might not have killed them.

"Union is a very small community," notes Rodriguez, "where everyone knows everybody else's business. If you sneeze, dammit, the sheriff lives two houses down.

"If everybody knows your business, do you want to deal with, 'Oh man, she gave up her children.'?"

Leaving the kids on the courthouse steps, as one neighbor suggested, was not an option. Neither was shipping them off to David. That is, not if Susan wanted a shot at snaring the man of her dreams.

Still, Susan's predicament was no different from that of thousands of stressed-out and lonely mothers who wouldn't dream of killing their children to make their lives easier. What separates the Susan Smiths from the rest of us?

Some therapists take a woman's word for it when she says her child would be better off with God than with her. One popular psychological term is "boundary confusion"—it suggests a woman starts out intending to kill herself. Unclear on where she ends and the kids begin, she winds up murdering the little ones.

The FBI researchers' position on all that is perfectly clear: These mothers are in denial.

Consider Susan's handwritten confession. It is riddled with attempts to rationalize or even excuse her crime.

"My children, Michael and Alex, are with our Heavenly Father now, and I know that they will never be hurt again."

"That's major denial," insists Rodriguez.

"I felt I couldn't be a good mom anymore, but I didn't want my children to grow up without a mom."

"I was an absolute mental case."

"What she's saying is, 'What I did was disgusting and heinous, but it wasn't me who did it. I was taken there by circumstances beyond my control. I wasn't myself. I was hurting. The person who did that wasn't the real Susan Smith.'

"These are the excuses and the denial."

In any case, many mothers who take that drastic, final step give out warning signals well ahead of time. Some complain about not being able to cope. Others express their stress in a physical manner. Many dead children first suffered beatings for years, and many of their parents had brushes with social-service agencies whose interventions fell short of saving the kids. But Susan Smith gave out no signals that she was having trouble. In fact, everyone in Union thought she was the perfect mother.

What is it that separates the Susan Smiths from the millions of mothers who find solutions to their problems other than murder? If we could identify that spark, that single ingredient that turned an average, normal, well-adjusted woman into a killer of innocent children, it might help society pick out potential killers before they take that final step.

Unfortunately, all the data in the FBI computer

and psychological literature combined is only useful in finding the murderer after the fact. The component that makes a woman kill remains the unfathomable mystery it was during the time of the Greeks.

14

The Lake

Damn, you're right. That is Oprah!

—Woman on a pilgrimage to Smith boys' death site
spotting a celebrity, November 5, 1994.

David Smith Sr. opened the door of his son's place at the Lake View Garden Apartments complex. The one-bedroom dwelling, just big enough for a newly minted bachelor with two little boys, was jammed beyond capacity with ashen-faced adults. Food baskets, their colored cellophane wrappings still intact, lay untouched all over the kitchen and dining room tables.

Not in any mood to mince words, David Smith Sr. cut to the chase. Without hesitation, he told me what no one else in his son's apartment would dare say aloud about his daughter-in-law.

"She deserves to die."

Father and son have quite a bit in common. Both men are small-boned and slight, with blue-green eyes that warm up engaging smiles. On the afternoon I met him, David Sr. clung to his good humor—it was only polite. The Smith men have this habit of submerging their darkest feelings while taking care to comfort the very people who are trying to console them.

Still, there was no pushing the issue of the day out of thinking range. Death was the subject on the forefront of everyone's minds. Susan's death, that is.

On Saturday morning, the two David Smiths met with Solicitor Tommy Pope of South Carolina's 16th Judicial Circuit, which covers Union and York Counties. The meeting was friendly but its purpose was bleak: Pope needed to decide whether he would ask a jury to make Susan Smith the first woman in forty-seven years to be strapped into South Carolina's electric chair. It was a decision, however, that Pope did not care to make alone.

So he asked father and son, Do you want to see Susan die?

David Sr., a Navy veteran with an agnostic streak, answered Pope with an emphatic, "Yes."

"I think she should get the death penalty," he told me. "It was just a senseless, senseless, brutal murder."

David Smith Sr. faced death in Vietnam, and he wasn't about to turn and run now. Thoughts of his grandsons' last, frightful moments alive strengthened his resolve.

"She drove those two children into the lake without so much as giving them a sedative—she did not put them to sleep first," he said, his eyes drifting off into the distance and landing on the far-off lake.

David Sr. wore blue jeans and a trim, white T-shirt decorated with a cable car and the words *San*

Francisco—his current home. He and his wife, Susan, had already spent two weeks in David's apartment, accompanied by David's manager at the Manteca, California, Wal-Mart where he worked. Until this day, the word *death* was never mentioned in the crowded apartment as everyone concentrated on bringing Michael and Alex home, alive. All that changed after Susan's confession.

"Who even knows if she really said, 'Good-bye'?" the grandfather said bitterly about Susan. "Whatever she said, I wouldn't believe it."

Grief welled in David Sr.'s throat as he contemplated his own loss. He still smarted from the death of his older son, Daniel, three years ago, and his breakdown shortly afterward. Now this.

"All I know is, I used to have two sons, and now I have one. And I used to have two grandsons, now I have none."

In a turn of events no one could possibly have foreseen, David Smith, father and son, were now being asked to decide the ultimate fate of another human being—one they knew and loved. Now that he held the power of life and death in his hands, David Smith Sr. discovered that his fervent desire for Susan's demise was the minority opinion.

That made matters tough for Tommy Pope, a man who believes South Carolina's electric chair is fearfully underutilized. What's more, Pope's position in the Smith case was complicated by a ticklish fact: The family of the crime victims and the kin of the killer were all the same people.

On Friday, Pope felt duty-bound to pay a call at the home of Susan's parents, Linda and Beverly Russell. He was accompanied by the woman in charge of Union County's victims' services program.

By coincidence, Pope knew Bev Russell; he'd run

for the office of Solicitor as the Republican candidate, and Russell was a bigwig in local party circles. But now, Russell was keenly aware that the same no-nonsense, law-and-order stances that once attracted him to the young lawyer were going to be used to prosecute Russell's stepdaughter for murder. In fact, Bev Russell knew that the man who stood in his doorway could be the person responsible for putting Susan to death.

All that went unsaid as Pope knocked on the door at Mt. Vernon Estates. The prosecutor expressed his condolences for the Russells' loss, and made a vague offer of assistance, but his reception was decidedly icy. Pope was out the door within fifteen minutes.

Pope's meeting with David Smith Sr. and family was far more cordial than his session with the Russells, but no less confusing. Pope did not come away with the clear-cut decision he'd asked for. That is, David's family did not, as Pope had hoped, lift the life-or-death decision from the prosecutor's own shoulders.

David Sr.'s wife, Susan, opposed capital punishment on principle, and she made no exception in this case. His daughter, Becky, the dead children's aunt, also had problems with the concept of execution. David's mother, Barbara Benson, a Jehovah's Witness, thought it best to leave the matter to the proper authorities—in this world and the next.

"Justice will be done," she told me confidently.

As for Michael's and Alex's father, it was far too early for David Smith to focus on his wishes for Susan. As the hours led up to his sons' funeral, David spent much of his day locked in the bedroom, staring at photographs of his boys, memories of their last moments together playing over and over in his mind.

He saw them on a Sunday, two days before the children disappeared. As the boys played in David's apartment, the father brought out a set of wooden blocks. Michael meticulously arranged the colored objects into a stack. Alex, baby that he is, sent it crashing to the floor. Michael built the pile back up, Alex pushed them down again. The guys played this game for a long time, laughing their heads off all the way.

It still hadn't sunk in. David did not fully realize that he would never see his sons again.

In his bedroom, David also wrestled with his feelings for the woman he married. He still loved her; David couldn't help it. He wanted badly to talk to Susan, to understand why she killed their children. Perhaps something happened to Susan. Maybe she wasn't responsible.

"I have no opinion," David said on the subject of Susan's execution. He was not going to be the man to pull the lethal switch.

Over the weekend, David accepted visits from two ministers, local men who thought they might help ease his aching soul. As the rest of the family sat quietly in the living room, the men sat with David in his bedroom. There, they promised David he would indeed play with his children again, in heaven.

It only made David sadder.

"I don't want to see my sons later," David told his dad. "I want to see them now."

For the grandfather, the hardest part was dealing with his son's inability to accept the events of the last two weeks.

"Why didn't she just return them to me?" David asked his father repeatedly. "I would have taken them." He could not dislodge this thought from his brain.

As he sat with his son, David Sr. flashed back on his own final visit with his grandsons. It was during a visit to South Carolina the previous February. Susan and David were still living together at the time. Alex was six months old. Michael, then two, ran all over the house. His grandfather delighted in chasing after him.

"He called me Gran," David Sr. remembered. "I was his Gran."

Like his son, David Sr. is not a man prone to emotional outbursts. But now, he could not stop the tears.

"They were good boys," he whispered. "I miss them so much."

Traveling by car and by truck, from nearby towns and far-away cities, they arrived on the shores of John D. Long Lake.

The visitors came from as close as Union and as far as North Carolina and Tennessee. As they approached the lake's glassy surface, nobody had any idea what he expected to find. A strange, potent attraction drew them to the spot where Michael and Alex breathed their last gasp. They just had to see.

The lake sits off a small road just off two-lane Highway 49, a few minutes' drive out of Union. You can't miss it.

On an autumn day, the lake's lovely serenity strikes the uninitiated as an obscenity, in contrast to the awful events that unfolded on this spot. Approaching the lake, the first thing a visitor sees is the boat ramp where Susan sent her sons to their deaths. The ramp, built of white gravel and concrete, slopes downward from the grass before ending in the cold, murky water.

Individually or in small groups, they all walked down the ramp—mothers cradling children, fathers smoking Marlboros. Eyes stared as if in a trance at the lake's luminous surface; legs seemed propelled, as if by themselves, to the water's edge.

Blacks and whites came out to stare at the lake alongside one another, all smarting over the loss of the little boys. All eager to toughen the bonds with their own children.

Flowers, cards, and teddy bears were scattered all over the shoreline. Balloons protruded from the surface of the lake. By Saturday, the lake was no longer a spot for fishing or a picnic, but a shrine to the dead.

"Sleep well in peace," read a card attached to a small bouquet of flowers, sent to Union by someone in Minneapolis.

"The angels will protect you now."

The visitors did not seem sure of exactly what drew them to the water, but once they arrived, all were glad they came. Danny Monroe drove an hour from Charlotte, North Carolina, to visit the lake with his sixteen-month-old son, Nicky. Monroe agreed to take full custody of Nicky when he split up with the boy's mom. The recent events in Union solidified his feeling that he had made the right choice:

"For the last couple of days, I just felt a lot of hurt. Something dragged me down here to get closer to my son.

"It's almost like an awakening. It's a fine line between being civilized and anarchy. People never imagine what someone can do to kids.

"I just had to see this. I needed to come down and see for myself."

Each visitor to the lake experienced his awakening on deeply personal terms. For the most part, people stared quietly, hugging their children, lost in thought.

Others were gripped with rage when physically confronted with the cold, wet place where Michael and Alex died.

"I'm angry, very angry," said Lucille Smith (no relation). "The way she lied and said a carjacker did it. They ought to tie her hands and put her in there. She oughta pay.

"They should drown her in boiling water. I want her to suffer. If you kill her it would be over, just like that," Lucille said with a snap of her fingers.

Lucille's train of conversation was picked up by a man named Robert Shetley, who knew Susan slightly through a mutual friend.

"They oughta put her in the car with a half hour's worth of oxygen," he suggested.

Tuesday Brown chimed in, "She should come down here and they should put her in the water, and take her out and put her back in again. She needs to suffer."

They stood at the lake, topping one another with torture techniques. Nothing, it seemed, was awful enough for Susan Smith. Not after what she'd done to them all.

"The devil got ahold of her," reasoned Sharon Glenn. "She needs to be caned."

As we spoke, a van appeared at the lake, and out popped none other than Oprah Winfrey, followed by her entourage. Dressed in a tan wool sweater and leggings, an outfit more appropriate for Chicago snow than South Carolina sun, the top-rated TV talk show host scrunched up her sleeves as she looked around.

For a long while after I mentioned Oprah's arrival, no one at the lake noticed her. Suddenly, one woman looked up, and made the connection.

"Damn, you're right," she declared. "That *is* Oprah!" Celebrities aren't often spotted taking the waters in Union, South Carolina.

Abruptly, everyone at the lake ceased talking, stopped what he was doing. In seconds, the star-struck throng formed a wide circle around Oprah and crew. The shoreline, crowded moments earlier, was emptied in favor of this new attraction.

That afternoon, Oprah was scheduled to tape her show at the church where Michael and Alex's funeral was planned for the next day. Finally, Union had something to talk about that was bigger than the children's death. Oprah was here! Donahue was on the way. The circus was in town.

When, the grieving people wondered, will it ever leave?

Employees at Holcombe Funeral Home on Union's South Street exchanged nervous glances when David arrived. He carried with him two little suits for his sons to be buried in. Apparently, David wasn't aware of the bloated condition in which his boys were found. Funeral home workers promised him they would do what they could with the suits.

From morning to night Saturday, van loads of flowers arrived on the funeral home's doorstep. Floral arrangements were sent from mourners in Connecticut and Florida, from Kentucky and Alabama and California. David Smith's family even received a message of condolence from a family in Australia.

The flowers and plaques, stuffed bears, and toys threatened to take over the entire Victorian mansion in which the funeral home was housed. Employees stacked them to the ceiling in one, two, then three of Holcombe's elegant rooms.

"God's little angels," read a huge card that was crafted completely from flowers. Another grouping centered on two large, wooden hobby horses.

In the home's largest and airiest room, the coffin holding Michael and Alex rested on a platform. The boys lay in a single casket of white, polished wood, bordered with gold. Their heads were placed at opposite ends. To the coffin's side, an easel stood, supporting a huge portrait of the little boys, together in life. Before the coffin and easel were dozens of pews, providing enough room for several hundred well-wishers. It would not be enough.

David dropped off the suits, then left the funeral home, planning to return in the evening to receive visitors. But on Saturday afternoon, he decided it was time to get some air.

For the first time since Susan's confession, David visited his co-workers at Winn-Dixie. Afterward, he took a stroll on Union's Main Street, accompanied by his uncle, Doug Smith, who was down from Michigan. In baseball cap and blue jeans, David looked a decade younger than his twenty-four years. Even so, a sharp-eyed CBS-TV reporter spotted him walking purposefully along the sidewalk, and ambushed David with a camera.

Walking briskly, David told the crew that he wanted to thank everyone for their flowers, cards, and letters of support. But David was clearly uncomfortable with the fact that the streets of Union were no longer his own.

"It's going to take a long time to get back into the groove of things, but I will," he added, refusing to respond to questions fired at him about whether he ever suspected Susan of murdering the children.

That night, David's uncle tossed out ideas. Should we issue a statement? Hold a press conference?

What will it take to make all these damn reporters go away?

In the afternoon, at the cemetery behind the Bogansville United Methodist Church, there was much work to be done in preparation for Sunday. Four huge, strong men were busy digging graves with the help of a backhoe.

The job was not a simple one. Before Michael and Alex could be put to rest, they had to move the grave of Daniel Smith, David's brother, to a roomier spot where he could be close to his nephews. David wanted it that way.

The men were accustomed to hard, lonely work in a setting most of us find depressing, but this job proved harder than all the others. They spent what felt like an agonizingly long time digging these graves. Thoughts of the children who would rest in this spot filled their minds.

"We don't bury many little kids," said one of the gravediggers, a man accustomed to dealing with untimely death.

"Everyone's cried over this one."

In the evening, all of Union and places beyond arrived on the doorstep of Holcombe Funeral Home.

The line of visitors extended from the spacious, pew-filled room where Michael and Alex were placed, then snaked through anterooms crammed with flowers before spilling out into the parking lot. As the temperature dropped close to the freezing mark, folks waited on line, illuminated by the lights of TV cameras, for up to two hours.

Inside, David Smith stood in front of his sons'

casket, and forced a smile for the thousands of people who came to say good-bye to Michael and Alex. Many of them had never even met the boys in life. In a dark suit, his sons' picture pinned to the jacket along with blue ribbons, David stood with his uncle, father, and stepmother on one side. David's girlfriend, Tiffany Moss, the Winn-Dixie cashier of whom Susan was so jealous, set tongues wagging by standing glued to David's other side, near his mother and sister.

"Thank you for coming."

David hugged each person who stopped by, sending many into tears. Once again, it was David who wound up comforting the same people who tried to make him feel better.

When he wasn't bravely greeting guests, David rubbed his sons' coffin and ran his fingers gently along their two-dimensional photograph. At times, David's smile evaporated. Overcome with grief, he broke down in tears, and relatives brushed his hair and caressed his back. David always recovered quickly. There were so many people to see. Holding a tissue tightly to his eyes, David made it through the night.

"I thought I knew her," he said at one point to his family. It was the only time Susan's image would be evoked. This was a time to think about Michael and Alex.

Mourners who kept up a courageous facade for David's sake lost it the second they hit the parking lot. The sight of David standing strong near the photo of his children was almost too much to bear. Exiting the funeral home, women and men, black and white, hugged one another in tears.

"We just couldn't get no peace until we came," said Michael Toney, holding his two-year-old son.

Toney and his wife Roxanne never met the Smiths, but they made the two-hour drive from their Anderson home to say good-bye to Michael and Alex.

"I have not stopped crying," said Joyce Bobo, who lives in Union. "I feel like if I could get up on top of a hill and scream, maybe I'll be all right. But it's going to be a long time."

Stacy Hartley, Susan's childhood friend, was one of the few who asked people to find it in their hearts to forgive Susan. Eyes puffy from crying, Stacy implored the mourners to recognize that there once was good in Susan. She called on the so-called God-fearing citizens of Union to leave the rest to their higher power.

The grief that took hold of the Holcombe Funeral Home that night did not stop with the mourners.

Standing behind yellow police tape outside the funeral home, a line of photographers was having trouble focusing. A man I know from New York, a video photographer who's built like a Mack truck and has more homicides under his belt than most people have socks, stood behind the line sobbing openly.

The camera crews stood in the cold until past midnight, when David's uncle, Doug Smith, emerged from the home to address them.

"The flowers, the number of people are overwhelming," he said appreciatively, making sure to mention that David thanked everyone for their kindness.

"He's a very young man, it's a very heavy load," David's uncle said.

He talked about David's earlier cruise through town, and said his nephew intended to go on with his normal life, right here in Union.

David remained in the funeral home nearly two hours after the scheduled 10 P.M. cessation of visiting hours, making sure to greet every person who came to see him. Then he escaped the crowd outside by sneaking out through a side door. It would take a while longer before life could go back to normal.

Much later, after everyone left the lake, a solitary figure approached the water. He was small-boned and slight, and so very, very sad.

The pull to the water was a force that could not be ignored, and David Smith was not immune. He, too, was drawn to the shores of John D. Long Lake, to the spot where his two little boys spent their last moments of life.

He just had to see.

15
The Saddest Day

The land cannot be cleansed of the blood that is shed therein, but by the blood of him that shed it.

—Numbers 35:31.

On Sunday morning, the rain came. Not the brisk, cleansing shower some people secretly wished for, but a dank and chilly drizzle that doused and then receded in fits and starts, like the gnawing pain that grabbed the townsfolk by the pit of the stomach. On this gloomy day, Michael and Alex Smith were to be laid to rest.

For Union's many churchmen, the most difficult task of all was at hand, and it was not saying good-bye to the little boys. The men of the cloth felt the need to urge their flock to forgive Susan Smith. For the people of Union, forgiving the killer required more strength than anyone felt he could muster.

Healing the rifts in the community would take even longer.

The day of mourning did not begin in the ordinarily lily-white environs of Susan's favorite church, but in a house of worship that fills each Sunday with an exclusively black congregation. The service at St. Paul Baptist Church was billed as a community forum for healing.

Pastor A. L. Brackett beseeched congregants to dig into their hearts to find compassion for Susan. And he called on them to praise authorities for refusing to persecute Union's blacks. While torn up by the tragedy, members of the black community felt vindicated by the white mother's confession.

"There was a sense of relief that it was not a black man" who did the killing, said Brackett, "and it is sad that a black image had been created in the minds of the community."

It was the Reverend James W. Richards who urged the audience to put aside their own complaints and remember the people who suffered most dearly from Susan's crime.

"Those kids are dead," Richards said. "David lost his children and his ex-wife in one fell swoop.

"David stood with his arm around a woman he trusted only to find out that she was the culprit. To add insult to injury by trying to call this a racial incident would be obscene."

The forum at St. Paul was well-attended, but not everyone who was invited showed up. Sheriff Howard Wells and his wife were the only whites in the audience. The others saved themselves for the day's main event.

Over at the Buffalo United Methodist Church, the crowd grew so large, employees erected speakers in the basement and set up another pair outside. The little brick church, sitting under the shadow of Buffalo's seemingly ubiquitous textile mill, was the site where, just a few Sundays before, parishioners greeted Susan and her beautiful boys, Michael and Alex. Too young to fully appreciate that morning's sermon, the boys squirmed in the hard, wooden pews, as Susan shushed them gently.

On this dismal day, the boys returned, without their mother, to the only church they'd ever known.

The Methodist church in Buffalo is an understated structure. Its hard pews are uncushioned; the ceiling and walls of the main sanctuary are constructed of plain brick supported by rough-hewn wooden beams. Not one rendition of a suffering Jesus hangs from the walls. It exudes a moving spirituality just the same.

The church's altar sits before an imposing, stained-glass window formed in the shape of a cross. On Sunday, as the rain slowed to an intermittent sprinkle, rays of sun sliced into the church. For the dejected congregation, that was an uplifting sign.

Hours before the 2 P.M. service, mourners arrived from points near and far. They squeezed their bodies tightly into the pews and filled up the folding chairs set in the aisles, until the only space left was out in the hall. The majority of the crowd was white, but many blacks sat among them, their clothes adorned with blue ribbons identical to those of their white neighbors.

Shortly before 1 P.M., the single, white coffin containing the bodies of Michael and Alex was rolled into the building on a gurney. Beneath the church's gigantic windows, the white box looked so very small.

An enormous spray of yellow roses spilled off the top of the casket, while two smaller bouquets of red ones were placed on either side, along with plaques bearing the dead boys' names. The portrait of Michael and Alex was taken from the funeral home, and placed on an easel beside the coffin. For more than an hour, mourners walked up to the altar, single-file, to stare at the photograph and touch the little casket. It was their last chance to connect with Union's lost boys.

Then David Smith arrived, and everyone gasped.

David woke up Sunday unable to walk unescorted. In a black suit, his face a lined mass of pain, the man who welcomed visitors so warmly the night before entered the church hanging onto the shoulders of his stepmother, Susan. His own legs looked as if they would buckle under his meager weight.

Tears streaming down their faces, close friends and family of David and Susan filled up nearly half the church. Relatives of David's sat peaceably along-side Susan's kin. David, however, seemed completely unaware of his surroundings. Sick with grief, he buried his head in his hands and cried.

David's agony was too much to bear. The sight of him crying triggered a spontaneous chorus of audible sobs, which reverberated throughout the building as one person after another let go. A few minutes later, the organist started playing "Jesus Loves Me," and four ministers took positions on the pulpit. This church contained far too much grief for one minister to handle.

"We have plumbed the watery depths of despair," the Reverend Mark Long began. It was an unfortu-nate choice of words to begin with. If anyone noticed, no one dared acknowledge it.

"Sometimes God takes from us the most pre-cious jewels in life so He can give them back to us in eternity," the Reverend Doug Gilliland soothed, taking on the role of healer.

"Forgive her," he implored.

The Reverend Dr. Joe Bridges smiled and spoke of the peace Michael and Alex were enjoying.

"They're having a great time with the Lord," he said. "They're having a grand time."

"Michael and Alex are home," added the Reverend Bob Cato. "I like to think of them sitting in the lap of God."

One minister managed to draw pleased nods when he suggested that, with the funeral, the media throng would surely soon pack up and leave. The others did their best to paint a serene picture of contented children, well cared for in heaven. And they spoke of the reunion the boys would have with their families in the hereafter.

But on Union's saddest day, all the prayers in the universe could not erase the pictures that burned into the minds of audience members. Try as they might, the people of Union could not let go of the vision of two little boys, suffering and screaming for their mother at the moment of death.

And nothing the ministers said could quell David's tears.

I don't want to see my sons later, I want to see them now!

David's anguished words of the day before lay heavily on his father's mind. David was inconsolable.

During the service, an infant, too young to know he was at a funeral, started squawking loudly. His mother tried rocking him, then feeding him a bottle before she gave up and left her seat, baby in tow. Even the most impatient adult didn't seem to mind the child's outburst, though. The sound of a child, healthy and alive, was by far the most comforting noise to emanate from Buffalo United Methodist Church during the entire forty-five minute service.

And when it was over, David walked alongside the coffin of his sons, this time leaning heavily on his mother, Barbara Benson. The rain had stopped, but David didn't seem to care. He led the pallbearers, most of them young men David's age, to a hearse. One of the men helping to carry the boys was Mitchell Sinclair, Susan's old friend.

The press, for the most part, gave David a wide berth. One TV producer, however, seized the opportunity to hand the grieving father his business card, along with an offer to appear on his show. David crumpled the card and hurled it to the ground.

Shaking visibly, David climbed into a limousine, surrounded by his own family as well as by Susan's mother and stepfather. Once inside, he buried his head in his hands for the journey to his sons' grave. Behind the limo, an unbroken line of cars extended the entire seven-mile route from the church to the cemetery.

The walk from the limousine to the grave site seemed to last for miles, but it really was only a matter of yards. On legs of jelly, David propelled his body to a chair set up for him under a tent, where he could see the headstone marking the grave of his brother, Daniel.

David's head sunk to his knees, and he let out a wail of pure pain. For a moment, it appeared as if he wanted to enter the earth himself.

As his sons were lowered into the hole in the ground, David moaned a single word, over and over and over again:

"No! No! No! No! No!"

*   *   *

Susan Smith's name was never spoken. As her sons were bid farewell in the church she'd attended since birth, and buried near the spot where she was married, Susan remained on suicide watch behind bars, seventy miles away in Columbia.

Joseph Workman, a local lawyer who's represented the Russell family for years, said Susan had been the subject of numerous death threats. But the vile letters and menacing phone calls never reached Susan. That was the plan. At the women's correctional center where she was held, Susan was labeled a "safekeeper." The perfect isolation in which she spent her days and nights was supposed to be for Susan's own safety.

As the Smith boys' funeral procession played on television sets everywhere, Susan Smith's cell stayed quiet. She ate her meals off a tray in her six-by-fourteen-foot world, and used its exposed sink and coverless toilet. Unlike other prisoners, Susan was not allowed outside; it was a security thing. She had no access to newspapers or magazines. She was not exposed to radio or TV.

Every fifteen minutes, a guard made note of her every movement, making sure the prisoner didn't try to hurt herself. Susan just sat on her cot in a paper gown, staring out the tiny window, thumbing the Bible she kept close to her heart.

News of her sons' funeral was broadcast world-over. But Susan Smith was the only person alive who couldn't have had a clue what day it was in Union.

Forgive Susan Smith? That message was the domain of church leaders. And of course, their media equivalent, the talk-show hosts.

Phil Donahue swooped down into South Carolina

after the funeral. High-profile tragedy makes for good ratings.

At a taping at the University of South Carolina, Donahue put together four people who believed Susan Smith should be given a break. One was the Reverend Bob Cato, who begged for her forgiveness at the funeral.

"I come from the side of forgiveness and grace, that this small town can go on," Cato said. "There are a lot of people that are angry and the God I quote a great deal says it's okay to be angry as long as you keep it under control."

But one audience member grew weirdly contentious while insisting that Susan was worthy of the community's love:

"We're a Christian community and I'm proud to be a part of Union and if you can't forgive Susan—I know it's a horrendous thing that she did—but if you can't forgive her, God'll never forgive you for anything."

Said another:

"God is a forgiving God. God is love and the devil's the opposite—hate. And if we of the community would pull together and pray for each other every day and pray for Susan, pray for her family and David's family . . . "

One man, Craig J. Richard, who served as Union High School's student body president in Susan's day, couched his religious convictions in philosophical terms:

"I loved Susan then, I love her now. We cannot hate Susan because of what went on. Right now, Susan needs us. She needs our support and so does the family and David. We can't hate her. And what we are doing is trying to convict her. It's our job to forgive.

"We call ourselves a Christian community, but as

Christians we are supposed to forgive. I don't see forgiveness here."

But underneath the vaguely threatening religious entreaties, a note of honest, persistent disgust shined through. It said, We are not like Susan Smith.

"Phil," said one woman, "I've been married and divorced and remarried. I've been separated. I've got three kids. I've had my power cut off, my water cut off.

"I've seen hard times, and I've never thought of killing my kids."

Then, there was the question posed by a black member of the audience, one the whites would prefer not to consider:

"Had it been a black man, would we be saying, 'Let's pull together and forgive each other?'"

And so, Union aired its gripes and prejudices under the national spotlight. No longer a sleepy, crime-free town, Union took on the role of microcosm of all the ills of society. What place could hold up under such scrutiny?

At Buffalo United Methodist Church, the Reverend Mark Long watched Union's transformation with dismay.

"It's almost as if our privacy has been invaded," he complained.

He hadn't seen anything yet.

Like all else in this case, the news spread quickly.

First, a TV network reported the rumor that a second arrest was expected in the Smith boys' murder case. Names of possible suspects jumped to the lips: Tom Findlay? Mitchell Sinclair? David Smith?

The other piece of news was a bit more believable.

Newsweek magazine issued a press release announcing a shocking tidbit on the Smith case included in its cover story, entitled "Sins of the Mother," due out on the stands the next day.

Quoting an unnamed police source, the magazine reported what Susan Smith saw after she set her sons adrift in John D. Long Lake.

The bombshell passage read:

"Smith told investigators that Michael, buckled into his car seat, woke up and began to struggle. 'He was struggling in absolute terror for his life,' the official told *Newsweek*, citing Smith's conversations with police. Smith, standing at the water's edge, watched and did nothing."

The account was immediately refuted by Susan's lawyer, David Bruck. "Susan never saw any of that and she never told anyone that she did. That account is simply made up," Bruck said.

Of course, there was no second arrest in the murders of Michael and Alex. Authorities simply wanted to determine if Susan told anyone about the slayings, before or after she committed them. The TV account was wrong.

As for the *Newsweek* story, Susan's lawyer continued to deny the account flat-out. But that story had a way of sticking with people.

In most ways, Bruck certainly was right about the story. It was dark at the lake on the night Susan murdered her children. It is unlikely Susan could have seen Michael struggle for his life in the sinking car.

So if one or both of the children did put up a fight during their slow, cold descent to the bottom of the lake, he did so on his own.

16

The Ultimate Penalty

Nowhere fries 'em quickly enough, not if you want to use the electric chair as a deterrent. You don't spank your children twelve years after they misbehave, especially if you want your other children to take note.

—Union County Solicitor Tommy Pope discussing the death penalty, November 23, 1994.

I feel more strongly now than I did [before] that the death penalty system, if you can call it a system, is so random and arbitrary that it has a ghastliness about it that no murder could ever equal.

—Defense lawyer David Bruck discussing the death penalty, *The National Law Journal*, June 6, 1983.

Capital punishment is an institution that at once fascinates and repels. We strain to hear the condemned man's last words. The contents of his last meal. Last rites. The last-minute phone call to the governor.

Death row is a culture unto itself, a mostly male society in which prisoners turn to God, stick their noses deeply inside law books, or engage in bizarre practical jokes. Why not? inmates figure. What can they do to us now?

A story making an orbit around death row in Florida's aptly named city of Starke a few years back tells of a black, male prisoner who engaged in a trans-Atlantic postal romance with a Frenchman. The inmate, a convicted rapist and murderer, was careful to conceal both his identity and his crime from the suitor. Instead, he told the ardent European that he was a white woman sentenced to die for killing her cheating husband in the heat of passion.

The inmate's payoff came on the day the Frenchman arrived at the prison gate, arms loaded with packages of lacy lingerie and flowers. The would-be lover was crushed when authorities took him aside and broke the news that the joke was on him.

For more than three decades, death row has been a secure, if not always raucous, environment for criminals to live out their days. Thanks to a cumbersome appeals process, hungrily taken advantage of by devoted antideath defense lawyers, most inmates spend a decade or more in prison before execution—that is, if the punishment is meted out at all. The same legal process that keeps condemned men alive in their cells also results in the reversal of a great many death sentences on technical grounds.

But in late 1994, change wafted through the dank air of the death house.

During the first week of December, five people were scheduled to die in legal executions across the country—a new record in the modern age of the American death penalty system. The milestone came a month after an Election Day in which Republican candidates swept contested seats across the country on platforms heavy on law and order. Just hours after winning a surprise victory over antiexecution maven Mario Cuomo, New York's newly elected Republican governor, George Pataki, talked about jump-starting his state's electric chair, which had sat in mothballs for decades.

But December did not turn out as bloody as capital-punishment enthusiasts hoped. By the end of the first week, two of the five men scheduled to die were still breathing. The nation's executioners fell short of their previous weeklong record of four state-inflicted killings—but certainly not for lack of trying. Boosted by a public fed up with crime, officials throughout the nation immediately focused their energies on streamlining the clunky death process.

Considering that more than 2,900 inmates live on death rows coast to coast, the national execution rate is actually quite puny. Before Christmas 1994, some 257 people had met their demise in electric chairs and gas chambers, on the business end of a hypodermic needle, or swinging from a hangman's noose, since 1976—the year in which America's dormant death penalty was reborn.

In that year, the U.S. Supreme Court lifted a fourteen-year moratorium on executions and decreed that it was indeed Constitutional for state governments to dispose of their hardest criminals in a permanent fashion. Today, the United States stands alone among Western industrial powers in taking advantage of its right to pull the switch or depress the plunger on its bad guys.

But all states are not created equal in their zeal to kill. Whether a convict winds up behind bars or strapped in the electric chair has a great deal to do with the location in which he murders, rapes, or ravages innocent people.

South Carolina is among a handful of states, mostly in the South, that lawyers refer to as forming the Death Belt—a region whose boundaries correspond, more or less, to that other well-known zone, the Bible Belt. Politically and morally conservative, the area's powers-that-be are not squeamish about putting to death their dregs of society. And they do it far more efficiently than their Northern neighbors.

Only twenty-four states have put to use their death-penalty statutes during the last eighteen years. Four states—Idaho, Maryland, Nebraska, and Wyoming—shipped just one person apiece to the hereafter since 1976. On the other end of the death spectrum, Texas, the Death Belt's shiny buckle, legally killed eighty-five inmates before the end of 1994. Florida was a distant runner-up, filling thirty-three coffins.

In contrast to the big death states, however, South Carolina ranks among those that inflict the punishment sparingly; just four inmates were executed since 1985, the year the state's laws were revised to meet the Supreme Court's new death criteria. The last time "Old Sparky," as the chair is known, cranked into action was back on September 6, 1991, when Donald H. "Peewee" Gaskins, a fifty-eight-year-old convicted serial killer condemned to death for killing another prison inmate, had a lethal jolt of electricity pumped through his body.

As 1994 drew to a close, and Susan Smith contemplated the very real possibility that she might become the first woman executed in her home state since 1947, South Carolina's electric chair had sat in the Broad River Correctional Institution in Columbia—just a few hundred yards from Susan's cell—like an unused piece of furniture for more than three years.

Death row is a cosseted world, whose citizens speak an arcane lingo and live by rituals unknown in the outside world. In this exclusive club, new members quickly learn to live by the rules—no matter on which side of the bars they reside. On rare occasions, though, outsiders are allowed a glimpse of life inside the death house. For me, that came in 1986 when, as a legal-affairs reporter for the *Tampa Tribune,* I traveled to the rural reaches of Starke to watch a man's life end under the white heat of 2,000 volts of electricity.

An execution is an extraordinarily scripted event; death row officials want to make sure that nothing is left to chance. Before the inmate begins the slow stroll from his cell to the waiting arms of the electric chair, each step is written out on paper. During the countdown that precedes E-Day—Execution Day— prison authorities rehearse their roles in a series of dry runs, timed to the second on a stopwatch. The inmate has work to do as well. He puts his affairs in order, picks his last meal off a menu, and selects the clothing in which he wants to be buried.

It was a chilly April morning in Starke when officials sat us down—journalists, disinterested witnesses, and law-enforcement officials—for an hour-long briefing in a room whose walls were painted a sickly shade of peach. The exacting, second-by-second choreography of the coming execution wracked our nerves even more than thoughts of the event we knew was to follow.

People in the death business work hard to make

executions appear ordinary and routine—and inmates for a while seemed to go along with the program as well. At the time I traveled to Starke, condemned prisoners felt honor-bound by a jail house pact: They gave no pre-execution interviews and made no displays of emotion. No cries for mercy rang out of death row. Instead, proud prisoners simply swaggered into the death chamber, sat down, and read their last words. The men's behavior was as predictable as their exact times of death.

On this day, though, all that changed.

Standing behind a thick pain of glass, we watched as the condemned prisoner, Daniel Morris Thomas, a thirty-seven-year-old black man, was led into the death chamber by a guard. His head was shaven and smeared with conductive gel in advance of the electrodes that were to be secured to his temples.

Ten years earlier, in a crime wave all but the victims had long forgotten, Thomas and his gang of thugs donned ski masks and waged a reign of rape and murder through rural central Florida. Entering homes through unlocked windows, they held entire families hostage. Drano down the throat was a favorite torture. Thomas was sentenced to death for shooting a Polk County man five times with a shotgun on New Year's Day, 1976. The last thing the man saw before he died was Thomas raping his wife.

Thomas's face betrayed no sadness as he swaggered into the room, and even less remorse. He approached the electric chair.

Suddenly, he forgot the script.

"Get off me, motherfucker!"

It was not on the agenda, but the inmate started to fight. Fists flying, legs kicking, Thomas started swinging at the warden and his aide with all the force he could muster.

"Get off me, *motherfucker!*"

A stream of obscenities penetrated the witness's side of the supposedly soundproof glass, as Thomas fought mightily for his life. There was no fear in the man's eyes, just naked rage. And something else: the will to survive.

As we watched, horrified, the man kicked a guard in the groin and knocked the telephone connected to the governor's office out of the warden's hand.

"This isn't supposed to happen, is it?" asked a young reporter, terrified Thomas might escape.

Even in the carefully ordered realm of death row, some things cannot be predicted.

We watched as four additional guards stormed into the death chamber. As one man pinned down an arm, a leg broke free and started kicking. Once that leg was secured, Thomas let loose with jabbing elbows. It went on like this for seven, incredibly long minutes. Finally, the six exhausted guards managed to strap down all of Thomas's athletic limbs. Normally, it takes one man thirty seconds to put a convict in the chair.

Even after Thomas's circulation was nearly cut off under the tight leather straps, he tried to bite the guards. Finally, the warden threatened the inmate with the only thing he had left to use against him: Stop fighting, he said, or you won't get the chance to read your final statement.

It seemed to work.

Reading from a yellow legal pad, the unrepentant murderer who fought so ferociously for life declared himself a "human sacrifice" in the political ambitions of Florida's then-governor.

"Governor Bob Graham . . . has made it perfectly clear to all politicians that the best way to win a political race is to boast that he will carry out the execution of every prisoner on Florida's death row."

The man was so out of breath by the time he quit struggling, we barely understood a word he said.

A guard covered the inmate's face with a leather mask. The executioner, his identity concealed by a black hood with cut-out eye holes, like something out of the Middle Ages, peered out from behind a blue curtain. In a moment, the warden waved his hand. The executioner nodded once, drew back the curtain, and pulled the switch.

There was no puff of smoke. No acrid smell. Just the silent, imperceptible passage of a man from life to death. The whole thing was over, as scheduled, in two minutes.

For most people on either side of the issue, executions exist only in the abstract. Strangely enough, watching the process in all its horrid imperfection has left me with no clear-cut answers as to whether it's wrong or right for the state to take a life.

Why did this man fight? Did he believe he could escape, or did he act on gut instinct? The answer died with him. Perhaps he simply felt he had nothing to lose. He might as well go down fighting.

But it is his defiance in the face of death that those of us in the witness room will always remember—and not the people whom Thomas killed, raped, and maimed for life. Because in the cosseted world of death row, where inmates outlive their victims by decades, the death penalty has little relationship to a crime, other than to satisfy a general public thirst for retribution.

And this is where people like Tommy Pope and David Bruck come in.

One has chosen to spend his life fighting to avenge the victims of crime—swiftly and completely, before they are forgotten.

The other has made it his life's work is to shine a light on death row, exposing what he considers the horrifying, capricious, and unfair manner in which this nation puts its criminals to death.

Perhaps the most interesting feature of South Carolina's electric chair is the clever way its designer ensured that no one knows who is directly responsible for snuffing out the life of the condemned inmate. In the executioner's room, located next to the death chamber, three red buttons protrude from the wall; each button sits on its own small, metal box. "All three buttons are capable of sending power to the chair, but only one is active during an execution," explains a handout distributed by the state Department of Corrections' press office.

Around midnight on the day of an execution—an event always scheduled, for some reason, at 1 A.M.— the inmate eats, showers, has his head and right leg shaven, and dresses in trousers whose right leg is cut off at the knee. Conductive gel is smeared on his head and leg, electrodes are attached to his body, and the inmate is strapped into the electric chair. A few final words, and a guard covers the man's face with a leather mask. It's time to roll.

Meanwhile, three Corrections employees, all volunteers, gather in the executioner's room; each is stationed at one of the three red buttons. When the warden give the go-ahead, the three executioners push their buttons simultaneously. No one is told which of the buttons is active. The executioners will never know for sure whose button sent the lethal dose of electricity coursing through the electrodes attached to the condemned man's head and leg.

South Carolina's deep-seated ambivalence over exercising its Constitutional right to take a human life is not reflected in the state's death-penalty statutes.

But it is a theme that crops up constantly in practice. And that is a weakness that men like David Bruck devote their careers to exploiting.

South Carolina's death row isn't a row at all, but rather a horseshoe-shaped block consisting of two tiers of cells, forty-eight per floor, overlooking a common day room. Each one-person cell measures seven-feet, eight-inches wide by eleven-feet deep, with nine-foot-high ceilings. And, as described in the Corrections Department's intricately detailed literature, "The cells are painted a light beige trimmed in dark brown. The ceiling is painted white. The floor has vinyl composition tile of a brown color."

The numbing uniformity of the death house is broken by the line of television sets suspended just outside the cells, spewing out soap operas and game shows morning until night. This beige-and-brown world, infiltrated by TV happy talk, is home to fifty-nine inmates, all of them men; twenty-eight are black, thirty-one white.

Death row is noisy. The sound of TV is nearly drowned out by metal gates, whose constant clang signifies the comings and goings of guards and inmates. Unlike the tension that often permeates maximum-security prisons, however, the cacophony of death row is punctuated with spirited banter. In their mutual incarceration, inmates and jailers can develop relationships more intimate than those existing among people performing ordinary office jobs.

And these relationships are longer-lived than those among most coworkers on the outside: Two men have lived on South Carolina's death row for seventeen years; two others have been condemned for sixteen. Such longevity is of relatively recent vintage, and for that you can thank men like David Bruck, a tireless advocate who has fought battles on behalf of the condemned all the way to the U.S. Supreme Court. Sometimes, he wins.

But until the case of Susan Smith fell into his lap, Bruck had yet to lock horns with Tommy Pope, a lawyer who's as passionate on behalf of victims as Bruck is about the welfare of killers. In the next few years, the course of the lives of the men in the cramped and clanging death house will be determined in large part by which man's world view prevails.

South Carolina's electric chair has certainly seen busier days. It was first plugged into existence in 1912, replacing a piecemeal system in which prisoners were hanged by the neck in individual counties. For most of its tenure, the chair was used primarily to punish black men: Of the state's 245 executions in the last eighty-two years, 195 of the dead were blacks, electrocuted for rape, murder or a now-archaic statute called "assault with attempt to ravish"—something like attempted rape—which, in practice, carried the ultimate penalty exclusively for black men.

The average age at execution is twenty-eight. The oldest person ever to be executed in South Carolina was Charlie Smith, a black murderer who died at age sixty-six on November 11, 1946. The youngest was fourteen-year-old George Stinney Jr., who died on June 14, 1944. Stinney confessed he bashed in the skulls of two white girls, aged eleven and eight, after he tried, unsuccessfully, to rape one of them. An all-white jury sentenced the teen to death after ten minutes of deliberation.

As with most modern executions, though, memories of Stinney's sickening crime were all but blotted out by the severity of his punishment. Newspaper accounts at the time of the execution related how prison guards had trouble strapping the five-foot-one, ninety-five-pound boy into a wooden chair built for adults. To this day, Stinney's death is cited in arguments against executing minors.

The 1940s were also the decade in which two women—the only females ever to be electrocuted in South Carolina—took their seats in the electric chair; one was black, the other white. On January 15, 1943, Sue Logue, a forty-three-year-old white schoolteacher from Lexington County, was executed for hiring a cousin to shoot the owners of a mule that had kicked to death a calf owned by her family. The last time anyone in a skirt sat in the chair was on January 17, 1947, when Rose Marie Stinette, a forty-nine-year-old black woman from Florence, was put to death for murder.

The chair was unplugged in 1962, and it sat quietly for the next twenty-three years. But even now, with capital punishment once again in fashion, getting the death seat back into action has proved a slow and laborious task. It is perhaps no accident that since 1985, all four inmates executed in South Carolina have been white men. Death-penalty foes, armed with reams of data, argue that the chair isn't color-blind. For reasons of race, or reticence, or mere technicality, Old Sparky no longer hums like he used to.

And that frustrates men like Tommy Pope no end.

Pope, a cocky and lanky six-foot-four, likes to call himself "one of the good guys." At a time when capital punishment is a subject cloaked in euphemism, the hard-as-nails prosecutor invokes a wickedly humorous candor on the subject.

"Nowhere fries 'em quickly enough, not if you want to use the electric chair as a deterrent," Pope told me, when I asked about South Carolina's dearth of death.

"You don't spank your children twelve years after

they misbehave, especially if you want your other children to take note."

But what to do about Susan Smith?

Deciding whether to seek life or death for Pope's most famous defendant is not a clear-cut choice. On the one hand, South Carolina law lists several aggravating circumstances for which the death penalty is deemed appropriate—including murdering more than one person and killing a child under eleven years of age. Susan Smith fits the bill in both instances.

However, execution is usually reserved for crimes committed against people who are not members of the killer's family—cases in which the perpetrator is considered at a high risk of killing again. Also weighing against Susan's electrocution is the fact that the victims' and killer's family are one and the same. Would the boys' father and grandparents only wind up doubly injured if Susan were to be killed, too?

The public at large, however, seemed uninterested in these fine distinctions, and calls for Susan's demise flowed through the prosecutor's office like electricity. Pope listened to the din and shrugged.

"It would be 2006 before they execute her," said Pope. "In this current state, it's a waste of time and money" to feed and clothe inmates, not to mention paying the staggering legal costs associated with executing them.

It's not that Pope lacks compassion. On the contrary, Tommy Pope is known around Union County for being as energetic in defending the rights of victims as he is feisty in pursuit of their tormentors. For the capital punishment fan, Pope is a regular pinup boy.

The son of a small-town sheriff, Pope was born with prosecution in his blood. When he was just eighteen, he was hired as an agent with the state's elite Law Enforcement Division—SLED. It was SLED's chief who suggested that the capable, young crime-fighter attend law school. He did, at the University of South Carolina.

The newly minted attorney quickly got a job with the Solicitor's office in Lexington County. When he was barely thirty, Tommy Pope ran as the Republican candidate for Solicitor in South Carolina's 16th Circuit, covering Union and York counties. When he took office in 1992, Pope became the youngest person ever to serve as an elected prosecutor in the state. Though he's been said to be a poor money manager—Pope got into a tiff with York County officials in early 1994 when his overworked office ran low on funds—his record in the courtroom is considered about as good as it gets.

In contrast to his shoot-from-the-lip style, Pope's colleagues call him a hyper-organized and sharply focused workaholic, a man who skips around his district carrying a thick, black loose-leaf notebook, which he refers to religiously. Like a very tall Boy Scout, Tommy Pope believes a lawyer must always be prepared.

Three months into office, Pope tried his first capital case, involving a York County man accused of breaking into the home of an eighty-six-year-old retired schoolteacher, sodomizing and beating her to death. The trial jury voted for the death penalty.

Of the other three capital cases tried by Pope's office during his first two years as solicitor, juries twice convicted the defendants of murder, but chose life in prison; in the last, the defendant pleaded guilty in exchange for life.

Before November 1994 rolled around, Pope thought he'd seen plenty of high-profile crime. In fact, on the afternoon of November 3, Pope had just won a conviction against a preacher who embezzled

$89,000 from his church, when the news of Susan Smith's confession permanently altered Pope's view of what a big-deal case looks like.

The news of Michael's and Alex's murders hit Pope hard. Like most people in these parts, the Smith boys' disappearance touched the prosecutor in intensely personal ways.

"I dreamed the first night or second night they were gone that they found them alive," Pope remembers. "A lot of people thought they were going to turn up, stashed away with a friend or in a hotel. Even now that we have the truth, the whole thing doesn't make much sense."

Pope says he will treat the Smith case no differently than any other. But the legal battle bears a cachet unlike any case he's ever tried. For one thing, the national media have been calling, threatening to turn the brash, young lawyer into a celebrity while he still holds the distinction of being the state's youngest prosecutor. All that's heady stuff. But it was Pope's five-year-old son, Logan, who brought home the importance of winning a conviction.

"Daddy, something awful happened," Pope remembers Logan telling him, as the tot watched news of the tragedy on TV.

How well Tommy Pope handles the biggest case yet to land on his desk will help shape the kind of world in which Logan Pope grows up.

In many ways, David Isaac Bruck, at age forty-five, is the older, liberal mirror-image of Tommy Pope. The father of a girl, age six, and a boy, four, the soft-spoken antideath maverick is, too, deeply concerned about the kind of world he'll bequeath to his kids.

A native of Montreal, Canada, Bruck enrolled in

Harvard in 1966, where he was active in the antiwar movement. Writing editorials against the Vietnam War for the *Harvard Crimson,* Bruck befriended the writer Michael Kinsley, CNN's generally left-of-center commentator. In an interview with his old college chum on November 26, 1994, Kinsley described Bruck as having been "widely regarded at the time as the nicest, most decent person in our crowd."

Asked Kinsley, "What's a nice, decent guy like David Bruck doing representing a woman who is accused of doing something that horrible?"

And, "Does it ever bother you that you might be putting back on the streets, or denying society's right to vengeance, against a person who has committed, in fact, a horrible crime?"

Even more to the point, Kinsley asked him, "These are people accused of horrible crimes . . . most of [them] have committed these crimes . . . and yet you're spending your life trying to save them from this punishment. And *you're not making as much money* as you could doing less controversial things.

"Why do you do it?"

Maybe it's the quiet, measured cadences of his voice, or maybe it's the face that has "decent" written all over it, but David Bruck sounded sincere when he offered this overworked reply:

"The most valuable thing in life isn't, I don't think, making more money as much as it is finding something useful and meaningful to do with your time. It's the time that's irreplaceable, and it will never come back and can't be amassed or put in your bank. And I just feel very lucky that I get to spend my time, my working life, helping people who are in terrible trouble, helping families who are in terrible trouble.

"And when people say, you know, 'How can you do this? What about the victims?' Well, my clients are parents and wives and husbands and children who have not killed anybody. They're not even accused of killing anybody, but they are hurting terribly. And they are victims of this process, too.

". . . I find it to be very rewarding work, and on top of that, there's the particular question of the death penalty, where a society is really hell-bent on making a God-awful mess out of tragedies and cases which are enough of a mess already. And to be able to put my shoulder to that wheel and try to be part of the minority, right now, of folks who are pushing the other direction—I think that's worthwhile."

If Tommy Pope is a capital punishment fan's sex symbol, David Bruck is its bogeyman.

Bruck was raised on pacifism just as his courtroom nemesis was schooled on police work. And it was those two, diametrically opposed preoccupations that led each man to a similar line of work on the same spot on the map.

After graduating from Harvard, magna cum laude, in 1971, Bruck enrolled in law school in, of all places, the University of South Carolina School of Law in the state's capital city of Columbia. At Harvard, Bruck had participated in antiwar activities near military bases, and tried his hand at community organization in Boston's blue-collar suburbs. He picked USC because it was close to Fort Jackson—a magnet for anti-Vietnam protesters.

After law school, Bruck accepted a job as a public defender in Columbia. After three years, however, "I felt I had learned the better part of what that job had to teach me," Bruck told *The National Law Journal* in 1983. So he settled in Vancouver, British Columbia, and became a welder. It was on a visit to South Carolina in 1980 that some lawyer friends gave Bruck a reason to stay in the South: They were defending a group of antinuclear protesters who were arrested at the nuclear dump in Barnwell, South Carolina.

Around this time, Bruck noticed that two black men who had had their death sentences overturned when he was a public defender were back in court for resentencing. He froze. "The whole bar of South Carolina knew that these men had not been well-represented" at trial, Bruck said.

His sense of moral outrage reignited, Bruck was reborn as an activist. Hanging out a shingle in Columbia, lawyer David Bruck declared war on the American government, fighting, tooth-and-nail, over its treatment of the people most folks refer to as the scum of the earth.

To Bruck, it's a matter of fairness.

In a 1981 article in the *Washington Post*, Bruck wrote that many of the men who drew their last breath in South Carolina's electric chair during the 1940s, when U.S. Senator Strom Thurmond, R-South Carolina, was a trial judge, would still be alive if today's laws applied. For one thing, blacks at the time were typically excluded from juries.

"Our country's sense of justice has changed in forty years and will no doubt change again," Bruck wrote. "The most up-to-date, safeguard-laden death penalty law may well seem as barbaric and unfair to our grandchildren as the trials [of the 1940s] do today."

And so, David Bruck turned his back on a lucrative career as a Harvard-bred private-practice lawyer to join a small fraternity of antideath ideologues, whose meager salaries are paid, for the most part, by government stipends. His efforts have saved the lives of men his Harvard classmates wouldn't dream of engaging in conversation.

In January 1994, Bruck argued before the U.S. Supreme Court that a man named Jonathan Dale

Simmons should have his death sentence overturned because a South Carolina jury had been tricked at trial into believing that, if they didn't pull the switch, Simmons might some day be set free on parole. In fact, Simmons, who was sentenced to die for beating an elderly woman to death and raping two others, was a three-time felon, making him ineligible for ever again seeing the light of day. Despite the jury's ignorance of Simmons's jailhouse prognosis, every court in South Carolina was content to see him fry.

The nation's highest court, however, sided with Bruck, and voted seven-to-two to overturn the man's death sentence. Bruck's victory did more than save one man's life. That ruling could result in a review of death sentences imposed in Pennsylvania and Virginia, as well as South Carolina—the three states in which juries are kept in the dark about a defendant's chances for parole.

In a scathing dissent, co-signed by Justice Clarence Thomas, Justice Antonin Scalia railed against this further erosion of the death penalty. The high court's "heavily outnumbered opponents of capital punishment have successfully opened yet another front in their guerrilla war to make this unquestionably Constitutional sentence a practical impossibility," Scalia wrote.

With Bruck leading the troops, the battle lines were drawn in Washington. But it took a woman to yank the killers' champion out of the relative obscurity of the courtroom and into the limelight. Her name is Susan Smith.

Soon after Susan confessed to killing her children, David Bruck received a call from Joseph Workman, a Union lawyer whom he'd helped five years earlier with a capital case. With Bruck's help, after three trials, Workman's client was sentenced to life in prison.

Now, Workman again needed Bruck's aid, this time to defend the daughter of two of his regular clients.

"Will you take the case?"

Bruck said yes. As usual, his fee would be discussed later. Susan Smith's mother and stepfather, Linda and Beverly Russell agreed to try to raise enough money to pay Bruck something close to what he is worth.

At the time Bruck agreed to defend the world's most hated baby-killer, it wasn't yet decided if *South Carolina* v. *Susan Smith* was to be a capital case. In fact, in its eighty-two-year tenure, Union is one of only two of South Carolina's forty-six counties that has never seen one of its convicts executed. Bruck wants to keep it that way.

"I can't honestly say that being exposed day in and day out to some of the ghastly things that people do to each other doesn't change your perspective," Bruck admitted a decade ago. "My heart doesn't bleed for murderers."

But, he added, "I feel more strongly now than I did [before] that the death penalty system, if you can call it a system, is so random and arbitrary that it has a ghastliness about it that no murder could ever equal."

Capital case or no, it didn't really matter. To David Bruck, defender of the indefensible, Susan Smith offered an unprecedented opportunity to tweak the system.

As 1994 drew to a close, Susan Smith, living in a cell at the Women's Correctional Center at the Broad River complex, spent her days and nights less than a quarter-mile from the death house that consumes so many hours of the lives of lawyers Tommy Pope and David Bruck. Already, their approaching legal fight was shaping up as a battle between the forces of dark and light. Of course, both men laid claim to the title of Good Guy.

17

The Living and
the Dead

*Manson probably had some problems, too. Everyone
must be crazy to commit these types of crimes.*

—Union County Solicitor Tommy Pope,
referring to convicted killer Charles Manson
to make a point about the insanity defense
anticipated in the murder case against Susan Smith.

For once in their careers, a couple of hotshot lawyers
decided to keep their mouths shut.

After *Newsweek* evoked the terrifying image of a
cold-blooded mother watching her three-year-old son
struggling for his life in John D. Long Lake—as she
stood on the bank doing nothing—David Bruck
released pieces of Susan Smith's handwritten confession to the media. Carefully selected pieces, that is.

"I wanted to end my life so bad and was in my car ready to go down that ramp into the water, and I did go partway, but I stopped. I went again and stopped. . . .

"I took off running, screaming, 'Oh God! Oh God, no! What have I done? Why did you let this happen?'"

Portions of Susan's statement were beamed around the nation with one clear intent: to show that Susan Smith was a remorseful basket case. She was not a mother who stood idly by as her child cried out for her to save him, the excerpts were intended to prove. Instead, she was shown to be a woman not in complete control of her actions. The leak was an attempt to put in motion the lawyer's arduous task of convincing people that Susan Smith didn't really mean to kill her two helpless children.

The battle for public sympathy had begun.

All this did not amuse Judge John Hayes, the man selected to preside over Susan Smith's trial. Judge Hayes did not want to see South Carolina's most celebrated criminal case turn into a media travesty à la O.J. Simpson, in which lawyers on both sides of a murder talk first to their favorite reporters, then, maybe, to each other.

In a forty-five minute conference call with Bruck and Pope, Hayes used his prominent position to issue a stern request: "Put a sock in it, will you?"

The men agreed.

So on Monday, November 8, with rumors about the case flying all over Union County, the lawyers issued a blanket denial: No more arrests were expected and no one had any knowledge that Susan watched her little boy struggle for his life. With that, they entered the cone of silence.

But not before Bruck again made headlines. This

time, the stories did not focus on any of the lawyer's actions, rather they concentrated on a subtle remark. Answering a reporter's question, Bruck merely said that a plea of temporary insanity was a defense tactic he had not ruled out.

"I'm going to consider everything," said Bruck. From the reaction, you might think he'd paraded Susan Smith around Main Street in a straitjacket.

Temporary insanity—or its technical term, diminished capacity—what other defense was there? The Smith case geared up at a time in which lawyers around the nation were having a field day defending the guilty with abuse-excuses. The legal art form is widely believed to have been born with the infamous "Twinkie defense," in which a lawyer claimed his client committed a crime because Hostess Twinkies played havoc with his blood sugar. More recently, a California jury deadlocked in the murder case against Lyle and Erik Menendez after the brothers testified that they shot their parents because they had been physically and mentally abused. Even ex-football star O.J. Simpson, who pleaded no contest in 1989 to a charge that he beat his wife, Nicole, claimed in a letter that he, in fact, felt that he was the abused spouse.

Susan Smith, on the other hand, was not a battered wife, nor did she fit the classic mold of a mother so stressed-out and abused, she felt compelled to lash out at someone weaker than she. Trying to prove she was prone to insanity, however, falls into the abuse-excuse category in one pertinent way: It suggests that she was not responsible for her actions.

But with all the people running around, claiming they were pushed into violence by forces beyond their control, recent public sentiment funneled into a resounding cry—Enough!

Tommy Pope isn't the kind of man to mince words when offering his opinion on the issue of criminal responsibility. Convicted murderer Charles "Manson probably has some problems, too," Pope told me. "Everyone must be crazy to commit these types of crimes. It depends what you mean by crazy."

Still, Bruck's task in defending Susan got a big boost from the accumulating stack of news stories, many of which speculated that Susan Smith's superficially rosy existence wasn't as perfect as it was cracked up to be. Susan had known death and pain in her young life. Her confession to murder can be read as an account of a botched suicide attempt.

But another reading of that statement gives a message that Bruck probably would have preferred for Susan not to have uttered aloud. The confession shows that Susan Smith, even though upset, was fully aware of her actions on the night she drowned Michael and Alex in the lake. And the ability of a defendant to understand right from wrong is a critical legal test for determining sanity.

And so, the case against Susan Smith appeared to boil down to a clash between psychology and politics: Will the shrinks conclude that a mother who drowned her boys had to be crazy to do it? And is the court of public opinion willing to give another confessed killer the benefit of the doubt?

Obviously, the news blackout in the case of Susan Smith could not last long.

On the Tuesday following Susan's confession, the media were still camped outside the Union County courthouse. David Smith decided it was time to get rid of the reporters once and for all. The only way to do that, he figured, was to give them what they wanted: himself. David Smith scheduled a date to face the horde.

But Tuesday turned out to be a bad morning for the bereft father. Plagued by swings of mood that ranged from numb to morbid, David woke up on Tuesday weeping for his sons. The noon press conference in which he was to speak was postponed to 1 P.M.

When the Smith family's car rolled up to the courthouse, however, David was not inside. Instead, David's father emerged from the car along with David's uncle, Doug Smith. The Smith brothers were joined by Susan Smith's brother, Scotty Vaughan.

Dressed in a blue chambray shirt and dark slacks, David Smith Sr., the neat, small man who looks so much like his son, approached the microphones and apologized that he would have to serve as a "poor substitute" for the younger David Smith. Head bowed with grief, voice perforated by sobs, the sad man who stood before the media was a shell of the angry grandfather who told me earlier that he wanted to see his daughter-in-law fry in the electric chair.

"I'm here on behalf of my son and my two grandsons," David Smith Sr. announced.

"On behalf of my son I want to thank everyone who's been so comforting and encouraging. The cards, letters have overwhelmed us." The elder Smith's face darkened. His son's difficult morning was at the forefront of his thoughts.

"This is more than one person can bear," he said of David Jr. "He's recovering from this tragedy in a very painful way. It's gonna haunt him for the rest of his life, I guarantee.

"He's not ready to face the public. He's still torn up and he's still hurt." The grandfather's voice cracked and his shoulders heaved. Just when it appeared he would have to stop talking, he pressed on.

"David loves each and every one of you. He's broken up. He wants his children back. That can't happen." It was too much to bear. Nearly choking on his own words, David Sr. forced himself to conclude: "May God bless all of you, okay?" Then he walked off, sobbing.

Scotty Vaughan, Susan's thirty-two-year-old brother, walked to the microphone next. A bearded version of brown-eyed Susan, Vaughan looked dazed and heartbroken over his nephews' deaths. Acutely aware that some folks might hate him just for being Susan's brother, Scotty was nervous as he approached the microphone.

Scotty began by thanking everyone for their cards and flowers. "It's unbelievable," he said. Then he got directly to the point: Please don't blame us all for Susan's sins.

"Many feel betrayed just as my family and David's family feel betrayed," said Scotty. "Me and my family and David's family needed your prayers. We are thankful to have people out there. Knowing you were there was truly a comfort for all of us."

Susan Smith should have been the one to say what came next. But Scotty, a truly decent sort, took it upon himself to make amends for the damage his sister's outrageous behavior had inflicted on the citizens of Union.

"On behalf of my family, we want to apologize to the black community of Union," said Scotty. "It's really disturbing to us that anyone would think it's a racial issue. My black friends called me and comforted me and told me they still love me. It's a terrible misfortune.

"Had it been a white man or a purple man or a blue man on the corner that night, that would have been the description that Susan used." There wasn't any man on the corner the night Susan killed her children, but Scotty's heart was in the right place. He concluded:

"We apologize to the black citizens of Union."

The next to speak was Scotty's friend, Sheriff Howard Wells. Unlike Scotty, Wells was a might defensive when addressing the race issue. He'd already made it well known that his deputies had been careful during the investigation to refer to Susan's phantom carjacker as "the suspect"—not the "black suspect." His department refused to harass Union's blacks. What more did anyone want? In every way, Wells believed, his men were sensitive to the feelings of Union's blacks. Those who would take issue with his department's actions, Wells insisted, were not from Union and had no right.

"Law enforcement would like to thank those who encouraged us. They were very helpful in our time of need," said Wells. Then Wells got to his point. Saying that he was pleased with Scotty's statement "because it was heartfelt," Wells added sharply, "The community at large has never seen this as a racial issue. There have been some individuals, but they were not representative of the community.

"I have no apology to make in any decision or any action I took."

Scotty Vaughan's apology, made at a time when his entire family was tussling with grief, was like a salve on the wounded feelings of Union's blacks. "The black community appreciated it," said the Reverend A. L. Brackett, pastor of the St. Paul Baptist Church, Union's largest house of worship attended exclusively by blacks.

"I was scared to death," Scotty, who was never much of a public speaker, told me later. "I hope it came out the way I intended it to. I guess it did."

Although Sheriff Wells didn't care to apologize, most of Union's blacks appreciated him, as well. On Tuesday night, about 200 people at an interracial community service welcomed the sheriff with a standing ovation.

A week into her captivity, Susan Smith was taken off suicide watch in the administrative segregation unit of the Women's Correctional Center in Columbia. Now, instead of a guard jotting down her movements every fifteen minutes, Susan's activities are monitored by an observation camera positioned permanently in her fourteen-by-six-foot cell. The room has a small, barred window looking out on the outside world, as well as another pane of glass facing inside the prison, upon which a guard's nose is likely to be pressed at any given time. Susan's cell contains everything a woman needs for day-to-day survival—sleeping bunk, toilet, and sink. She just never knows for certain when someone might be watching.

Being taken off suicide watch brought some new additions to Susan's wardrobe. Inmate Susan traded in her paper gown for a prison-issue blue cotton shirt and blue denim jeans. Three times a week, guards take her out of her cell, in leg irons and belly chains, then release her, naked, into the shower. Once a day, Susan is led in chains to a small outdoor yard with a cement floor. Under the watchful eyes of her jailers, Susan's chains are removed, and South Carolina's most famous prisoner is free to engage for one hour in what's known in the jailhouse as "exercise."

All that means is Susan is let loose in an empty, confined outdoor space. She is provided no exercise equipment, and no one to play with. "Basically, she can walk around," says Robyn Zimmerman, director of public affairs for the South Carolina Department of Corrections.

Save for the company of her jailers, Susan does

everything—eat, sleep, bathe, squint at the sun—all by herself.

Not counting her lawyer, whom Susan calls upon as needed, she is allowed to make two telephone calls per week. Susan has chosen to engage in short, tearful conversations with her mother, stepfather, and brother, who have remained loyal to her through thick and thin. Once a week, Susan's parents make the seventy-mile drive to the prison, where they sit with Susan, her handcuffs and chains removed, around a table in a small, depressing room. A guard watches over them every second.

Since her status was changed, Susan's possessions increased from her former cache of paper gown, eyeglasses, and Bible. Susan is allowed to possess such toilet articles as soap and shampoo. What's more, guards trust her to handle a pencil and paper, which she uses to write letters to her family in the same regular, schoolgirl script she has relied upon to jot down all the most important missives in her life, from her delight in giving birth to Michael to her confession to committing his murder.

Susan's keepsakes also include several photographs of her dead sons, which she keeps close to her bed. In the dull blur of the passing days, when the words of her Bible cease making sense, she stares at those sweet, little faces. Susan compulsively puts herself through this exquisite agony—constantly reminding herself of all that she threw away. Any feeling, even excruciating pain, is better than the dreary, beige-and-brown death that is Susan's life.

Susan is shown some of the mail that has poured into the prison, as well as to the home of her mother and stepfather in Union. Like everything else in her cell, the letters and cards, many containing Bible verses, are carefully screened. "We're praying for you," is a popular sentiment to come Susan's way. Under the watchful eyes of prison authorities, it would be easy for Susan Smith to believe she's captured the public's love and support. She never sees the other kind of letters, which outnumber the congenial messages many times over. "The electric chair is too good for you, bitch," is one popular refrain Susan never encounters.

Aside from these material items, Susan's only regular company is a television set posted down the hall from her cell, which blasts soaps and game shows, from morning until night, until it feels like a high-tech torture.

Not far from Susan's cell, in another part of the Broad River Correctional Institution complex, the condemned men of South Carolina's death row live their lives in very much the same manner. Only these men spend every day within feet of the state's electric chair. It may not be the country's most active chair, but the men are well aware that their odds for survival could alter drastically at any time. For that reason, the wooden death seat is kept dusted, wired up, and ready for use at a moment's notice.

With the same, exhaustive detail that distinguishes all its printed material, the Corrections Department explains, to anyone who cares, everything a reader could possibly want to know about the care and feeding of Old Sparky.

From the segment entitled "The Electric Chair and Execution Chamber":

"The execution chamber is 15 feet by 8 inches by 20 feet. The ceiling is 10 feet 4 inches high. The walls are brick and the floor is covered with a vinyl floor covering.

"The 40-inch leather chin strap goes around the condemned man's head and buckles behind the headrest to hold the head in place. A dark brown, soft leather hood covers the head and is tied in back. A ground wire runs from a conductive band around the right calf to a plug on the platform.

"There is a chest strap with a lap strap to hold the condemned man in the chair. These straps are 2 1/4 inches wide and 1/4 inch thick. . . .

"The warden has a direct phone line in the Capital Punishment Facility to the deputy commissioner for operations who, in turn, will be in direct contact with the governor's office during the period directly preceding an execution. Backup phones are installed to ensure system reliability." And on and on it goes.

Then, for serious technology buffs, there is a section entitled "Electric Chair Operations":

"Power to the chair is on an automatic cycle, activated when the active executioner's button is pushed. The cycle consists of 2,000 volts at five amps for five seconds, followed by 1,000 volts at two amps for eight seconds followed by approximately 250 volts for two minutes.

"There are three sources of power for the electric chair and death house. Either the building or the chair can be supplied from any of the sources independently. The power sources are S.C. Electric and Gas and two emergency generators installed permanently on SCDC [South Carolina Department of Corrections] property."

From her lonely cell in a segregated corner of the women's facility, Susan Smith can't see the wooden chair. But often she imagines the feel of its hard wood against her back, the grip of leather straps secured snugly on slender wrists. Like her children's car seats, once strapped in, there is no escape. That chair has a way of making its presence felt.

As the days ticked by toward Christmas, Susan Smith bided her time sitting on her bunk, her thoughts invaded by the sound of the television blasting down the hall. The noise haunted her. Susan tried to close her mind to the constant commercials for *Mighty Morphin Power Rangers* and *The Lion King,* for all the fabulous toys and educational games she should now be buying for Michael and Alex. Even in prison, the sound of happy children anticipating Christmas was everywhere; there was no blotting it out. So Susan Smith used the only tools she had available to combat it. She picked up her Bible, her newest and dearest friend, and started reading it, chapter and verse, out loud.

Louder and louder, Susan raised her voice. Soon, the only thing anyone could hear in the women's facility of the Broad River correctional center was the screeching symphony of metal upon metal, the urgent voice of the TV announcer, and the sound of a young mother praying to God to deliver her from living hell.

18
David

But now he is dead, wherefore should I fast? can I bring him back again?

—David, about his son; II Samuel 12:23.

"I don't hate Susan."

The words were spoken by the one man in the world whom even the most God-fearing citizen of Union might not blame for wishing Susan Smith dead. His name is David Smith.

In the dark days following his children's funeral, David begged enraged friends not to speak ill of his wife. Incredibly for a man who'd just had his entire immediate family wiped out, David expressed his continuing loyalty to the mother of his children—the mother who murdered his children.

"She must not have been in her right mind to have done this," David said in a phone conversation with Susan's older brother, Scotty Vaughan, a man with whom he'd always shared warm relations. "I don't hate her."

In a way, David's unbroken devotion to his wife brought him more pain than he might have endured had his emotions toward her blossomed into hate. In the days following Susan's arrest, David winced at the countless attacks leveled against Susan, all of them made with the best of intentions. David's friends assumed their sentiments would comfort David. They couldn't have been more wrong.

The people who cared about David needed to put themselves in his shoes. One day, David Smith was the loving father of two young boys, who had an estranged wife with whom he still shared warm feelings. The next day, he grew closer than ever to the woman he still loved as the couple banded together to search for their missing sons. Suddenly and without warning, David Smith's entire immediate family, the people he cared for most in the world, was taken away forever for reasons David could not comprehend. In a way, those who maligned Susan also took stabs at David's delicate emotions.

While David's parents remained cordial to Susan's family, they couldn't help but maintain a frosty distance from the people who raised their grandsons' killer. Any mail addressed to Susan that arrived at David's apartment was tossed into an envelope by David's father, who then shipped it without comment to the home of Linda and Beverly Russell in Mt. Vernon Estates. David, though, being the kind of guy who looks after others when he's dying inside, felt compelled to tell Scotty Vaughan that he bore no ill will—for his family or for Susan. Eventually, David felt the need to spread his message beyond Union.

Representatives from national news programs and tabloid TV shows were still lined up on David's doorstep. Some sent condolence cards, or flowers and gifts with notes attached, begging for interviews. Apparently confident that he could speak his piece—and reveal no more than he wished—David agreed to appear on the NBC program *Dateline*. The program aired on November 18, during the heart of television's all-important sweeps month, when viewers are counted and advertising rates are set accordingly. Katie Couric was the TV personality who scored what's known, in broadcast-speak, as "The Get." Perhaps David felt that Katie, herself the mother of young kids, would be sensitive to his feelings.

David's face was drawn and pale as he squinted into the camera lights erected in his apartment on the day the interview was taped. A deep drawl emanated slowly, deliberately from trembling lips as David weighed every word with extra caution. Katie pressed gingerly, prodding David to spill his guts. David's strained face was almost too painful to watch.

He described being called at work at 9 P.M. on October 25th, and rushing to the side of a weeping, hysterical Susan. In many ways, David was still at her side.

Katie Couric: What kind of mom was Susan?

David Smith: Susan, she—she was—she was great. She really was. She was a very dedicated, devoted mother to those two children. She would—you know, they—we—they were her heart just like they were mine. They were her life just like they were mine.

Katie whipped out a scrapbook, and she and David smiled together at the happy images of Michael and Alex playing in Dad's bachelor pad. In one touching shot, their little heads peeked out of a laundry basket.

Smith: You don't know how much they enjoyed a simple clothes basket together, how they would play in that clothes basket for hours and just—you know. But that's—that's them playing together in a simple clothes basket.

The snapshots started with the birth of the boys, and included all the important events of their young lives—birthdays, Christmas, the unwrapping of exciting new toys. There were plenty of shots of David playing with his kids, events immortalized by unseen hands. Was it Susan who held the camera?

Smith: Michael always enjoyed cutting grass with me. He loved to ride the lawnmower with me. He loved to be, you know, be with his daddy doing that.

In the next instant, Couric produced a shot of Susan holding an infant Michael in her arms. It wasn't clear how the picture of Susan got into the stack, but David grew visibly upset at the sight of it.

Couric: Hard to look at that picture?

Smith: Go on to another picture.

Couric: Don't want to talk about it?

Smith: Don't want to talk about it.

Katie ignored the request, and pressed on in the Susan vein.

Couric: You all spent a lot of time together during those nine, nearly ten days.

Smith: Yes, we did.

Couric: At any point did you look at her and ask her, "Did you do something to our children?"

Smith: No. No. I believed her 100 percent.

Couric: When she failed the lie detector test, did she come to you and say, "I hope you believed me. I hope you don't think that I'm involved?"

Smith: Yes, she did. She did.

Couric: She did? What did she say to you?

Smith: She just—you know, she said that she wasn't sure if she failed it. She said she believed from what they told her that she did fail it, and that she felt that they—that—that the local law force was starting to doubt her. But I never did.

Couric: Not for a fleeting instant?

Smith: Not for a fleeting instant.

David was asked how he felt when he learned that Susan confessed she murdered their children.

Smith: I was heartbroken. I was—it was a—a sickening feeling that I've never felt—experienced in my life before. I felt empty. I felt hollow. I felt betrayed.

Katie was finally getting somewhere. She swooped in for the kill.

Couric: How do you feel towards her now, David?

But David was ready for her.

Smith: I'm not going to talk about that issue. I don't feel comfortable talking about that.

Couric: Would you like to see her?

Smith: For sure. Yes I would.

Couric: Why?

Smith: Well, because I've got certain questions that, you know, need certain answers before I can have my own self peace of mind.

What those questions were, David wouldn't say.

David talked about his visit to John D. Long Lake, to see the place where his children died. "I had—I had—I had to see," he stammered. "I just had—I just had to take a look."

David's composure returned when he described his memories of Michael and Alex. As long as he thought about the good times, David felt as if his sons were alive again.

Couric: What do you miss most about the boys?

Smith: I miss those—those little smiles that they can give. They could take this whole earth and turn it upside-down. They could take your worst day of your life and change it—and turn it around, and make it— make the rest of it better, the rest of the day better, with their smiles.

Couric asked David about the picture of Michael and Alex he wore on his breast pocket.

Smith: It makes me feel closer to them, and also it's right in their place, where Michael and Alex will always be, which is right next to my heart. It's where they will always be for the rest of my life—will be in my heart.

Nothing succeeded in melting David's grief. Preachers only reminded him that heaven was his best hope for seeing his sons again. But how can there be heaven after a world in which mothers kill their own children?

David continued to spend hours locked away in his bedroom. His worried father postponed his trip back home to California, and spent most of his time in the living room outside David's door.

The bosses at Winn-Dixie, who hired David while he was still in high school and promoted him into one of their stars, respected his decision to stay home, and promised to hold the assistant manager's job open for him. After awhile, David talked about returning to work part-time. But it was still too soon to return to a normal existence, whatever that meant.

In his bedroom, with photographs and memories as his only company, David Smith was trapped in his own prison. A prison made even more terrible by the absence of bars on the windows.

19

Clash of the Titans

In a case of dissension, never dare to judge 'til you've heard the other side.

—Euripides' *Heraclidae*, 428 B.C.

Scotty Vaughan hadn't laid eyes on his little sister in more than two weeks. Three times, Susan had called him on the phone. Three times, they'd exchanged just a few, quick *I love you*s before quickly hanging up. But on November 18, Scotty made the hour-long drive from Union to the York County courthouse to see her.

In her prison blues, wispy hair swept up into a ponytail, Susan looked pale. Her eyes were puffy behind her wire-rimmed glasses, and her fingernails were bitten to the quick. But she was still Scotty's sister. She was still beautiful.

He threw his arms around her.

"We all still love you," Scotty said, tears streaming into his neat beard. "We're still behind you. We're gonna help you get through this."

The brother-sister reunion took place in a room adjacent to the main courtroom in York, where a hearing was scheduled in the case of *South Carolina* v. *Susan Smith*. Also exchanging hugs with Susan were her mother and stepfather, Linda and Beverly Russell. In the course of a few minutes, the family's smiles and tears got all mixed up. There was so much to say, but no words sufficed. To the loneliest inmate in South Carolina, the presence of her family was all that mattered.

"We're all standing by her," Scotty told me.

But all the family's support did nothing to negate Susan's predicament. Security was tight around the York County courthouse as the hearing drew near. Sharpshooters, an unusual sight in small-town South Carolina, stood at the ready to take out any troublemakers.

Susan was transported from her cell in Columbia to York on that Friday for a hearing on an urgent request filed by the prosecutor, Tommy Pope. Pope asked a judge to order defense lawyer David Bruck to hurry up and declare whether he planned to seek an insanity defense for Susan. That way, Pope could demand that Susan Smith be examined immediately by a state-employed psychiatrist—someone, Pope insisted, who might offer an unbiased opinion as to whether she was legally insane. According to Pope, there was no time to lose, not when Bruck's shrinks had unlimited access to the defendant.

"The defense has been talking to her from day

one," Pope told me in his indomitable style. "We don't want her to spend six months in insanity school before we get her to trial."

Pope had to convince the hearing judge, John Evans, that the examination was critical to the interest of justice. David Bruck, on the other hand, would fight Tommy Pope tooth and nail. In his effort to get Susan off the hook by any means possible, it was in Bruck's best interest to keep a tight leash on his client.

Some didn't need any convincing about Susan's mental state, however. Already, Susan had persuaded at least three people that she was quite insane when she killed her children. Her family would grasp at anything to explain how their beloved girl could do the unthinkable.

"The Susan Smith I know and loved could never do this," said Scotty. "She was not in her right mind."

In her confession, Susan tried to suggest that it wasn't really she who did the killings, but rather some alter-ego over whom she had no control. Her family supported this contention all the way.

"I don't hold her responsible," said Scotty. "She's pretty fragile.

"I just know that she, in her right mind, was not capable of doing anything remotely close to this." Then, Scotty threw in a surprising twist: "She's sad. She's heartbroken. She has hurt herself more than anybody."

Anybody, of course, except for Michael and Alex.

Susan's family had made peace with the hatred being flung in their direction. "One of the ministers we talked to kind of put that in perspective," said Scotty. "Those people expressing their hatred and having the negative attitudes, those are the people who need our prayers also. They don't know God's love and don't have Christian love in their hearts."

At this hearing, another reunion of sorts was about to take place. David Smith, the other man who loved Susan but hadn't seen her in more than two weeks, made the trek to York to watch the day's proceedings with his father and stepmother. Unlike Scotty, however, David did not appear in the anteroom to hug his estranged wife, nor did he declare his allegiance to her. The two never spoke. In fact, Susan didn't dare make eye contact with the man whose children she drowned. And David didn't push it.

The moment Susan walked into the courtroom, it was apparent to all who saw her that a new milestone had arrived in the public life of Susan Smith. As TV cameras recorded her every facial tic, Susan, for the first time ever, shed tears for all the world to see.

During all those press conferences she presided over during Michael and Alex's disappearance, Susan stammered and prayed and gazed sadly at the floor. But now, as David Bruck led Susan to a chair, his arm draped protectively around his client's shoulders, big, wet tears rolled from Susan's eyes and splashed off the table before her. Susan buried her face in hands tipped with painfully chewed fingernails, and continued to cry. All the tears that Susan had neglected to spill for her dead children now streamed between her fingers and left salty trails down her arms. When crying for herself, Susan seemed to have an endless capacity.

As Susan wept, Tommy Pope began the slow and laborious task of trying to pound the nails, one by one, into Susan's coffin. Of course, when it came to escaping from tight spots, David Bruck was a regular Harry Houdini. It was time to let the games begin.

Tommy Pope stretched to his full height and addressed Judge John Evans. Right away, the prosecutor produced a copy of Susan's handwritten confession—

the very document that Bruck released earlier in an effort to show that Susan was out of her mind. If that's the case, figured Pope, it's only fair that my psychiatrist have a crack at her. There was urgency in the prosecutor's voice as he took the podium.

"To begin," Pope said, referring to the confession, "she said that she was very emotionally distraught and she didn't want to live anymore. Later on in the statement, she said, 'I felt even more anxiety coming upon me about not wanting to live.' She stated at one point that she wanted to end her life so bad, that she was a nervous wreck, she was an absolute mental case. . . . "

Bang, bang, Pope banged away at the nails.

"Your honor, it is my understanding that from the time she was taken in until recently, that she has been on a suicide watch. There has also been indications that, I understand, in her past, that she has been suicidal. In addition, it is my understanding that Mr. Bruck, and certainly, properly, is contemplating, through what I've heard in the media, an insanity defense."

In the media. Bruck cringed as he heard his own ill-advised comment come back to terrorize him. He made a mental note to turn that one around in his favor.

"So certainly," Pope continued, "based on the crime itself, your honor, the statements that she has made and her history, it certainly warrants some indication or some reason to believe that she should be evaluated."

Pope was going great guns when Dr. Donald Morgan, a forensic psychiatrist retained by the South Carolina Department of Mental Health, took the witness stand. Morgan is a professor of psychiatry at the University of South Carolina School of Medicine and a director of forensic psychiatry training programs at the William S. Hall Psychiatric Institute.

Pope asked the psychiatrist to assess the importance of examining a criminal soon after she commits a crime.

"Well, the closer to the time of the incident that we get to evaluate the individual, the clearer our picture can be of the mental state at the day of the incident," Dr. Morgan testified. "So that is very difficult, sometimes, when we're asked two years later, in a very serious matter, to perform the evaluation because so many things have changed in the person's mental state. Some people have gotten sicker. And some people have recovered. And both of those could give us a lead as to an erroneous conclusion."

Judge Evans wanted to know if the stress of being in jail could affect Susan mentally. Dr. Morgan said yes, "particularly where someone has killed a loved one."

"There clearly are the stress of that loss, realization of what's been done. But, given that, the closer you can be to the event, the clearer your picture can be because the mental state can change, a person's defenses may change and we could err in either direction."

Then the judge asked if the videotapes made during Susan's preconfession press conferences were useful in evaluating her. Again, Dr. Morgan's answer was an emphatic "Yes," although that probably was not the answer that Pope, who wanted Susan on the psychiatrist's couch now, would have considered ideal.

Pope knows better than to declare victory before the last man is cleared off the battlefield. But at the start of the hearing, things seemed to be going his way.

"Your honor," Pope said, "based on Dr. Morgan's

testimony, and I think that's the issue—not, 'Could you do it later?' but 'What is ideal?' Because one of the purposes we have here is, obviously, to seek the truth. And if there's a determination of insanity, or whatever determination may be made, it is incumbent or proper for the court, for the defense, for the state— for everyone—to know what the true issue is, or what the true fact is in this matter."

Bang, bang, bang, bang, bang.

But then, a crack materialized in Pope's mighty delivery. Something suggested by Bruck nagged at the prosecutor, and he found himself on the defensive. Pope elected to pursue the matter head-on.

What Bruck had brought up was the fact that investigators, in their zeal to secure Susan's confession, did not take the time and effort to set up a video camera to immortalize Susan as she described how she drowned her children. While videotaping a confession is not required by law, the omission forced Pope to concede that "an opportunity was lost" for the prosecution to evaluate Susan's mental state. A videotape would have presented the state with a golden opportunity to examine Susan's unaltered visual and audio image at a crucial time. Now, two weeks after investigators blew that chance, Pope argued that every second that ticked by without an independent diagnosis of Susan's mental state was an egregious blow to the prosecution's case.

"The opportunity is here for Dr. Morgan, as soon as possible, in Ms. Smith's current state, to deal with her now," Pope said. "If we don't deal with that right now, then that opportunity will be lost. And so, as we continue to delay, more and more opportunities to seek the truth, more and more opportunities to get a true picture will be lost as this is pushed and as this is delayed."

Pope was treading water. Bruck came up to bat with an advantage. However, the defense lawyer still had a tough job ahead. Everyone in Union County was hanging on his every move.

"David Bruck is really caught between a rock and a hard place," Robert Fierer, a defense attorney providing commentary for CNN, said during a break in the proceeding.

"He knows that anything he does is being watched, so he has to balance a fine line where he tries to keep some privacy in his own examinations of her . . . Whereas, the prosecution is trying to force that issue so that they can let the [potential] jurors know just exactly where Susan Smith is."

David Bruck had to be brilliant. The stakes were too high if he failed. Silver hair conservatively trimmed for the occasion, Bruck began by saying that Pope had no right to demand that Susan be examined, based on nothing more than his hunch that she might plead insanity. This was no time for a dry legal argument, though. Bruck pulled out the violins, and played to the judge's heartstrings.

The lawyer got rolling with a little story about a condemned man Bruck represented during his appeal.

"I was there when his head was shaved and the conducting gel was rubbed in and he was taken off to be electrocuted," Bruck started, in his best low-key delivery.

"What happened in the case was that his public defender saw no harm in consenting to the very motion Mr. Pope makes today, because, after all, they probably weren't going to plead insanity anyway, so what harm would it do to allow the South Carolina Department of Mental Health have a crack at him?

"But two years later, when [the defendant] would

be resentenced before the jury of Horry County, one of the psychiatrists from the Department of Mental Health popped up at his sentencing hearing to give what could only be described as quack testimony, predicting as a matter of absolute certainty this man—who had never been violent a day in his life before the murders of which he was convicted— would certainly be violent every, single chance he got, for the rest of his life, unless he was executed. And that he personally derived sadistic pleasure from making people suffer and, in effect, the only thing the jury in its right mind could do was to order this man to be electrocuted."

Pop, pop, pop. All those nails Pope had banged in were flying out of Susan's coffin faster than the eye could see.

"Now, he had no warning that that's what could happen as a result of that evaluation in the South Carolina Department of Mental Health. And neither did his lawyer. And that is why he consented to it. And that is the testimony and that is what the jury heard and their verdict was death, and he is dead.

"Now, his lawyer can be forgiven for having made that mistake. But I am not going to make the same mistake."

Bruck was not a man to quit while he was ahead. So far, he'd managed to insert into the record a sympathetic tale about a murderer—prudently omitting any details of the man's crime. Now, he planned to pass all the goodwill he conjured up for the poor, executed killer over to the woman who sat at the defense table. The same woman who, at her own press conferences, earned the goodwill of all who listened by telling little anecdotes about her life with Michael and Alex.

"I'd like to tell you a very little bit about Susan,"

said Bruck. "She is, at this moment, very fragile. She is regressed. She is not able to protect herself.

"I live near a busy street in Columbia and there's traffic charging up and down it all day long and all night. I have a six-year-old daughter who could probably cross that street and get to the other side safely, if I let her do it by herself. But I would rather not let her cross that street without my holding her hand. Well, Susan right now is a lot like a six-year-old child. She cannot defend herself. She needs to be protected and she needs to be protected against the legal peril that I have just described for you."

Pop, pop. Bruck reached into his bag of tricks to retrieve the never-made videotape of Susan's confession.

"Now, the solicitor was saying that the opportunity is being wasted, this opportunity is being lost," said Bruck. "The opportunity that was lost by law enforcement can never be reconstructed, can never be regained. That is water under the bridge."

The moment arrived for Bruck to put a positive spin on one of his own earlier statements. Fortunately, this Harvard-educated native of Canada knew how to speak fluent South Carolinian.

"Mr. Pope said he understood, from the media, that I was considering an insanity defense. And I have to tell you, I certainly am learning a lesson in dealing with the media in the last two weeks. I didn't think that I was a complete *hayseed* about it, but I learned that I am!

"What he is referring to is the fact that I was asked whether I will mount an insanity defense at the one press conference I was foolish enough to give in this case. And I said, 'I've been on this case seventy-two hours, I'm not ruling out anything,' never imagining that the headlines that would emerge from that is, 'Smith Defense Considering Insanity.' Well, that's the press reports that he's referring to. I have not ruled out anything. I haven't seen the state's case. I have a great more work to do with my own client. . . .

"We are way ahead of ourselves trying to figure out whether there is a rush, a breakneck race for the state to have the best possible opportunity to rebuff a defense that may never be asserted. I simply suggest that we take things one step at a time."

From smoke and mirrors to brass tacks. Bruck breezed along, declaring that it was "unprecedented" for prosecutors to demand that a defense lawyer declare his intention to use the insanity defense—and give them a chance to psychoanalyze his client— twelve days after he takes on the case.

Then Bruck threw in his master stroke.

Bruck told the judge that he had asked, nicely, for Pope's office to provide him with a list of the last twenty cases in which prosecutors demanded a defense lawyer give them immediate psychiatric access to his client. Bruck also asked that, along with each such case, Pope's office provide the date of the defendant's arrest. Hey, said Bruck, if it's so normal for prosecutors to demand a defendant's mental evaluation the second there's any *suspicion* she might plead insanity, surely they can give me a list of twenty measly cases.

Of course, the prosecution provided no such list.

"Now, please don't misunderstand me. I don't mean this to sound like I am accusing the solicitor of doing anything improper," Bruck's voice positively dripped with sincerity.

"He has dealt fairly with me. He has handled this very difficult case in a most honorable fashion and I appreciate everything about his handling of the case up until now. But I do think that if it is true, the solicitor alone has the data to prove me wrong, I do think if they've never made a motion like this before, the things Dr. Morgan said are not scientific discoveries that were made yesterday, to the extent that they're true at all.

"If the state ever made a motion like this before, twelve days after an arrest in any case, and came into court to argue against defense attorneys and urge the instant evaluation . . . then the equities can't weigh as heavily on the state's side as they claim.

"Why, for the first time, now?"

The nails were not only out of the coffin, the lid was bursting open. Bruck went for the big finish. Stealing Pope's lead, Bruck claimed *his* method led to the truth.

"It's in Susan's interest for the whole truth to come out in this case. We are not going to be hiding anything. It is going to take time and we are dealing with things which are fragile as matters of the human mind and heart can be, and I just have to ask you to trust me when I tell you of the need to be careful, and the need to go slow. That's about all I can say."

Actually, Bruck had a lot more to say. He tried to suggest that any kind of examination by the prosecution's "hired gun" psychiatrist could be unconstitutional. It's not, said the judge.

The hearing concluded after Bruck asked Judge Evans to grant him another ninety days to review the prosecution's case against Susan Smith. In that time, he planned to decide whether to invoke one of two defenses—innocent by reason of insanity or guilty but mentally ill. Judge Evans said he would rule on the matter in ten days. That meant Susan would languish in jail for ten more days, at the very minimum, unseen by an independent psychiatrist.

Bruck's courtroom performance blew away the commentators.

"David Bruck has been very effective," raved attorney Robert Fierer. "He is a quiet, competent, careful lawyer. He's a persuasive lawyer. He is a person who appears to me to both know the law and understand how to present it to a court in the most palatable fashion for the court."

Echoed defense lawyer Herald Price Fahringer: "I must tell you, I'm extremely impressed with the way David is handling this matter. He's moving along cautiously, obviously choosing his words very carefully."

In the end, the judge sided with David Bruck. The attorney won another three months with Susan all to himself. The defense takes Round One on a technical knockout.

Of course, Tommy Pope had his own ace in the hole. In the coming weeks, he would decide whether to ask a jury to put Susan Smith behind bars for life, or put her to death in the electric chair.

There was no denying it. In this war, it was winner take all.

20
Moving On

OVERHEARD: A woman on a Brooklyn-bound R train, talking to a friend: "So, my daughter asks me, 'Why did God let that mommy kill her two boys?' And I say, 'Well, honey, God didn't have enough angels up in heaven, and they were so good and innocent, he had to take them.' So then she says, 'Mommy, if God needs more angels, will you kill me, too?'"

—*New York* magazine, December 12, 1994.

The last words spoken to me in the City of Hospitality were far from hospitable.

"How the hell can you write about someone you don't even know?" a woman demanded after I asked for her comment. It was clearly time to go home.

By van and by satellite truck, via puddle-jumper or nonstop jet out of the Greenville-Spartanburg regional airport, the press took a hike, abandoning the Deep South as quickly as we found it. We left Union behind, gratefully, taking with us nothing but a new set of war stories. But the Susan Smith case was unlike any other assignment the wisecracking horde had sunk its teeth into. We sensed it would stick with us long after the next grisly murder replaced it.

To this hard-boiled bunch, even the most horrendous explosion, mass murder, or natural disaster was fodder for twisted jokes in the playground we call a newsroom. And the gallows humor has a way of seeping into the culture at large. The massacre in Waco, Texas, cannibal-killer Jeffrey Dahmer—no story was too horrible when it came to providing raw material for the likes of *Saturday Night Live*. But the Smith case was the exception. No one, anywhere, had the heart to poke fun at a mother who drowned two such beautiful and innocent boys.

Stories about Union, however, were fair game, and reporters had a ball recounting personal horror stories to astonished friends in the big city. Like the one about the waitress at Union's Pizza Hut who, at the stroke of midnight on a Saturday, tried to wrestle a beer out of the hands of a six-foot photographer with a powerful thirst.

"It's Sunday!" the waitress shrieked, lunging for the beer. He dodged, she missed. When the photographer stared at the woman defiantly, refusing to give up the brew without explanation, she went wild.

"I could get arrested!"

"Do I have to pay for it?" the photographer asked, noting that his mug was nearly three-quarters full.

"Of course you do."

Before she could make another dive for the glass, he chugged it down, like a good New Yorker.

"Would you like anything else?" the defeated waitress asked icily.

"Yeah," said the victorious shooter, "another beer."

And then, there was the producer who stopped in K-Mart to buy a package of underwear at 1:15 on Sunday afternoon. In a hurry to make it to the Smith boys' funeral on time, he sprinted with his purchase to the nearest idle cashier.

"I'm sorry," the woman informed him, "the law prohibits us from selling anything but food until 1:30 P.M." She muttered something about how the guy was supposed to be in church, anyway.

"But you have to sell it to me *now*!" he whined.

Unable to chug a three-pack of Fruit-of-the-Loom briefs, the producer tossed the package to the floor and stormed out of the store empty-handed.

No one up North believed these tales the first time they heard them. But I swear they're true. I was a witness.

Ragging on Union was not meant to be mean-spirited. On the contrary, the laughs helped take some of the tension out of covering what represented one of the most difficult assignments in many of our careers. Sure, there are stories more horrible—wars and famines and natural disasters where body counts run far higher than the death toll in Union. But those tragedies often are relieved by accompanying tales of heroism and hope. There was no such relief in Union. The faces of Michael and Alex followed you everywhere. Reminders of their death were unrelenting. For days, we had lived a small town's agony, lost our objectivity as we wept at a funeral, and prayed for two little boys who didn't deserve what they got.

The woman who told me off was wrong. I did get to know the people about whom I wrote.

Once back in New York, it was amazing to see the extent to which people had internalized a killing that occurred more than 1,000 miles away. Even in a place like Brooklyn, where infanticide is hardly unknown, it was impossible to look at small children without imagining the features of Michael and Alex.

"She had a nightmare," a friend of mind said of her four-year-old daughter, who had watched a news account of the Smith case. "I've had to explain what happened to her very carefully." But who would explain it to the mother?

"God!" she said. "Why did she have to do that?"

Friends and acquaintances turned to me for answers, as if they believed spending time in Union was all it took to understand an incomprehensible crime. They wanted to hear that Susan Smith was completely out of touch with reality, but that simply was not true. Every other possible explanation—she wanted to get rid of her children to snag a new boyfriend, she was messed up in the head from her father's suicide—only made people angry.

"That's not good enough," they invariably argued when confronted with the potential reasons. "I would never kill my kids. Why did *she* do it?"

And so, Susan Smith was elevated from human being to symbol. Her name was evoked to epitomize evil in the same fashion that some people speak the name Adolf Hitler. She may be a girl from South Carolina, but something about her very existence bothered folks from all parts of the country, who followed the saga from day one.

Susan Smith's sheer *normality* was troubling. This was not some mad woman, but an ordinary person who never gave a clue as to what she was capable of. She could be any one of us, and that begged some difficult questions: What makes Susan Smith different from any other mother? Or, could *anybody* snap, just like that?

Another character in the drama to take some flak from the wider public was Union County Sheriff Howard Wells. Even thousands of miles away, folks were angry that the sheriff allowed Susan Smith to carry on her carjacking charade for so long. Nine days seemed an outrageous length of time for authorities to entertain Susan's lie and prolong the nation's agony. Didn't he know she did it? Fair or not, all of Wells's advanced law-enforcement training and professionalism couldn't shake the perception that he ran a sheriff's department in a Podunk town straight out of Mayberry, staffed by a crew of bumbling Barney Fifes. It made people feel better to see him this way. At least, they told themselves, the same thing couldn't happen here.

Or could it?

Single-handedly, Susan Smith helped renew the popular interest in capital punishment. In the electric chair–free zone of New York, people talked as enthusiastically about putting Susan to death as did their counterparts in Union. No one, however, made the point quite so colorfully, or controversially, as Scott Lobaido, an artist from the New York City borough of Staten Island.

Lobaido wanted to tell the world how he felt about the baby-killer from the South. So around Thanksgiving, the artist went to work—in a big way. He chose as his canvas a billboard overlooking Hylan Boulevard, Staten Island's main drag. On it, Lobaido painted the head of a woman; her face was unmistakably that of Susan Smith. Next to it, the artist depicted a disembodied hand holding a bloody knife that had just been used to cut the woman's head off. Below the graphic picture, Lobaido put the message:

"Susan Smith Murdered Her Babies. I Say Cut Her $#!@$#! Head Off!"

Maybe it was the billboard's prominent placement, in the line of sight of so many children, that was so upsetting. A slew of outraged Staten Islanders formed a picket line, and demanded that the gruesome work of art come down. The billboard was removed after just a few days, but not before it made its memorable point.

As Thanksgiving rolled around, few people in Union could find reason to celebrate. At the home of Linda and Beverly Russell in Mt. Vernon Estates, the days preceding the holiday weekend were particularly bleak.

The first blow to the peace came the Tuesday before Thanksgiving, when Judge John Hayes, acting on a media request, released the text of Susan Smith's confession to the public. Not just the carefully culled excerpts shared by defense attorney David Bruck, but the entire pathetic, self-serving speech. Susan's statement was broadcast worldwide instantaneously.

I felt I couldn't be a good mom anymore but I didn't want my children to grow up without a mom.

Why was I feeling this way? Why was everything so bad in my life? I had no answers to these questions. I dropped to the lowest when I allowed my children to go down that ramp into the water without me.

I love my children with all my heart.

For the first time, we got to see the little heart doodles Susan was so fond of drawing.

That will never change. I have prayed to them for forgiveness and hope they will find it in their heart [♥] to forgive me. I never meant to hurt them!!

Susan's convoluted logic for murdering her children—she wanted to commit suicide, but didn't want the boys to live without a mother—was a devastating insult to every parent who heard the confession. And her statement proved unequivocally that Susan was aware of everything she had done.

Within minutes of the confession's release, savvy court-watchers dissected Susan's words. The verbal math added up to a chilling equation:

- Susan Smith devoted just one-sixth of her two-page confession to apologizing for her crime.
- She referred directly to her sons' deaths just twice.
- She used the word *I* in her statement fifty-seven times.

Before the turkey could hit the table, even more traumatic revelations would shake the foundations of Linda and Beverly Russell's split-level house in Mt. Vernon Estates. On Thanksgiving eve, prosecutor Tommy Pope filed court papers to support his request that Susan Smith be examined immediately by an independent psychiatrist. Pope's brief, now in the public domain, set forth Susan's mental-health history, for the first time, in exacting detail.

Pope spelled out how, at age thirteen, Susan tried to kill herself, swallowing a large quantity of "aspirin and Anacin." Again, at age eighteen, said the court papers, Susan tried to kill herself with aspirin. That overdose landed her in the psychiatric ward of Spartanburg Regional Medical Center for a week, the papers said.

Susan's brushes with madness, until then mere matters of speculation and rumor, now were documented facts for public consumption. But the revelation

about Susan's forays into the medicine chest were not
the most horrifying news to sail through the airwaves
on the holiday weekend.

Several weeks earlier, media outlets had filed
requests, under South Carolina's public information
laws, for details of a sexual-abuse complaint Susan
was rumored to have made to authorities while she
was in high school. Sheriff Wells refused even to confirm whether such a complaint existed. So far, he had
succeeded in sitting on the media request.

But on Thanksgiving weekend, former Union
County Sheriff William Jolly confirmed that Susan
had, in fact, told her high school guidance counselor
that her own stepfather, Beverly Russell, molested
her, *The State* newspaper reported. Counselor
Camille Stribling dutifully passed the allegation along
to the sheriff's department, the former sheriff said.
But after an investigation was launched, said Jolly,
Susan had a talk with her mother, then withdrew the
complaint. With no witness and no independent evidence of a crime, the sexual-abuse probe was
dropped.

Of course, the newspaper took care to point out
how easily a girl who had sought attention by swallowing aspirin—and who grew into a woman capable
of lying for nine days about her children's kidnapping—could have made up a story of molestation in
another bid for the spotlight. Still, the six-year-old
complaint was out there now for everyone to read
and discuss. Nobody was very hungry on Turkey Day.

Linda Russell was always fond of cooking for a
crowd, and she did her best to live her life as normally as possible under the circumstances. She held
her head high while shopping in the local stores, and
continued socializing with friends and family. Real
friends don't abandon people in times of need, she

figured; Linda Russell had nothing to be ashamed of. This year, of course, no one had the strength to make a big to-do about a family holiday. For one thing, the dining room table would look that much emptier without Susan and David in their places, without Michael and Alex perched alongside them in high chairs.

But the family wasn't giving up on life entirely, and a small get-together was planned with just close relatives.

"I don't know if we can call it a celebration," said Scotty, "but we still have a lot to be thankful for. I still have my family."

And so they ate together, and rejoiced in the living.

Meanwhile, David Smith tried to get through the holiday as best he could. David didn't eat much these days, and his mother worried he'd never recover.

"Don't worry, Mama," he assured his mom, Barbara Benson. "It's not so bad."

In her cell in Columbia, Susan Smith had to make do without her mama's home cooking. She did, however, dine on institutionally prepared, processed turkey, reheated and slapped on trays for the enjoyment of the guests of the South Carolina Department of Corrections. Within sight of her photos of Michael and Alex, Susan read grace from her Bible, then picked at her plate. She ate this dinner, as she did all the others, alone in her tiny cell.

21
Susan

Leave her to heaven,
And to those thorns that in her bosom lodge,
To prick and sting her.

William Shakespeare's *Hamlet*, 1600–1601

"I have not turned against Susan. I love Susan."

Linda Russell was at home, cooking for company, on an early December morning when the telephone rang. After everything she'd been through—her daughter's arrest, her grandsons' funerals, and now, revelations about that dead-and-buried incest allegation against her husband—Linda Russell was understandably wary of strangers. For some reason, however, this morning found her in an unusually chatty mood, and she took a phone call from Susan Crimp, producer for the syndicated TV program *Hard Copy*.

"I love my daughter."

After enduring the back-breaking load of the last few weeks, Linda Russell braced this morning for more torment. Susan's lawyer, David Bruck, had called for a preliminary hearing in her murder case, scheduled for December 8 and 9. As anyone who followed the O.J. Simpson case knew, the "prelim" was something like a mini-trial. Testimony would be given by the cops who interrogated Susan, by the coroner who did the autopsy on the dead children, and by the divers who discovered Michael's and Alex's bloated corpses. For Bruck, however, the hearing offered an opportunity to win a peek at the kind of evidence the prosecution planned to use against Susan. If it helped her defense, everyone who loved Susan figured, maybe the ordeal was worth it.

But to save Susan's hide, would Bruck paint a hideous picture of Susan's family life? Would the lawyer dare bloody his own client's parents so that Susan might live? These worries were not mentioned in Mt. Vernon Estates.

Two days before the hearing was to begin, Linda Russell was busy, as usual, with her day-to-day chores. Hers was a religiously observant family; they figured God would take care of things. Life must go on. But the moment the subject turned to her daughter in prison, Linda's voice was commandeered by grief.

"Our friends are still our friends," Linda said, "and Susan's friends are still her friends." The mother paused as sobs wracked each sentence. It was hard to go on.

"I have not turned against Susan—Oh, heavens no! I love Susan. Nobody has turned against Susan at all."

Linda was asked if she believed something must have been terribly wrong with Susan mentally for her to kill her children. "That's absolutely true," Linda answered, and she cried again:

"I want people to understand that there's more to this."

But on this day, Linda Russell steered her energies toward her cooking. There was plenty of time to worry about her daughter.

"My life hasn't changed," she insisted. "Everyone is being supportive."

In the end, Linda Russell was spared the potential hurt and embarrassment of a preliminary hearing. At the last minute, David Bruck withdrew his request, and the event was canceled. Bruck gave no reason for dropping it. Quite possibly, the lawyer saw nothing to be gained from stirring up national publicity anew in a case that had fallen from the headlines—though not from public memory—everywhere except in South Carolina.

Union by now had become a permanent station on the ghoul tour. People from miles around drove to the town, making sure to stop at the intersection at Monarch where Susan claimed a black man took her car with her sons inside. The next stop on the journey was John D. Long Lake, where the many flowers strewn on the banks by mourners by now had wilted; blue and black ribbons were tattered around the edges. Tourists pulled up to the shoreline, took out cameras, and posed for snapshots. Not much fishing went on in that lake anymore.

Meanwhile, the wheels of justice clanked on. A grand jury was scheduled to hear the case against Susan on December 12. No surprises were expected to come out of their chambers. The indictment was merely the first step in the long and drawn-out process that could put Susan in an early grave.

"The prospect of an early death is not what is causing Susan the most pain right now," David Bruck said. "It is life that hurts her."

On December 12, the Union County grand jury, meeting in secret as always, returned an indictment for two counts of murder against Susan Smith. The process was a mere formality: Under South Carolina law, prosecutors present evidence to the eighteen citizens on the grand jury, at least twelve of whom must vote yes in order that formal charges may be brought against a defendant. An old courthouse joke says that any prosecutor worth his salt could win an indictment against a ham sandwich, if he chose to.

But three hours was quick. While it might not set any records, the relative haste with which the panel voted in favor of the murder indictments reinforced the notion that prosecutors had plenty of evidence to use against the confessed killer in a court of law.

It also meant that it was time, once again, for David Bruck to wax eloquent on behalf of his client.

This time, though, Bruck faced an unusually tough audience. The greater public was not as receptive to tales of a murderer's plight as the judge who agreed that Susan did not have to be examined immediately by an independent psychiatrist. Many members of the folks at whom Bruck aimed his comments would like nothing better than to throw the switch on the electric chair with their own hands. Luckily for the lawyer, Bruck was at his best when the odds were stacked against him.

On the Monday that Susan was indicted, the defense lawyer made himself available to reporters for the first time since Judge Hayes requested a news blackout in the case. Once again, Bruck painted a portrait of Susan as a helpless girl only vaguely aware of the events swirling around her.

Bruck mentioned the photographs of Michael and Alex that Susan keeps in her cell. "She thinks about them all the time," he said.

"During the day, she prays and cries. She dreams about them at night and the nightmares begin. Denial and shock are going away, and it is fair to say the full horror of what has happened is bearing down on her now."

Interestingly, Bruck, like Susan, referred to the murders as "what has happened"—rather than "what Susan did"—as if the children's deaths were some unfortunate but unpreventable accident. Susan Smith and David Bruck could learn a great deal from one another about verbal gymnastics.

Rather than stress the horror of the death penalty, as he did in court, Bruck's strategy when dealing with the media was to downplay its importance. Susan, he stressed, had long been suicidal, and as a young child she was forced to deal with her father's violent and untimely death. Bruck went as far as to say the topic of execution "seems irrelevant" in light of the awfulness of Susan's life.

"The prospect of an early death is not what is causing Susan the most pain right now," he said. "It is life that hurts her, not fear of death."

Bruck talked about the ever-present television down the hall from Susan, blaring children's toy commercials and Christmas specials from morning until night.

"They are more knives through the heart. She loved those children more than anyone. She is mourning her children, grieving for her children. She does not understand it any better than anyone else does.

"I know that may sound strange, may even make some people angry. She does not expect anyone to feel sorry for her, not now. But I wanted to say these things because this case has caused so much hurt and so much pain."

As usual, Bruck saved his master stroke for last. He told how Susan's mother and stepfather selflessly make the weekly trek to Columbia to visit their daughter. It is they, not Susan, who live in terror that Susan will "die a violent death at the hands of the state."

"They bear a far greater burden than human beings are designed to bear."

Kill Susan, he implied, and you kill off yet another member of a family that already has suffered such unimaginable losses. The lawyer carefully sidestepped all questions regarding David Smith's possible feelings on the subject.

Bruck also danced around questions about whether he would pursue an insanity defense. He was anxious to keep Susan out of the clutches of the state's psychiatrist for as long as humanly possible; David Bruck was not about to tip his hand now.

Bruck wanted to make sure that, aside from her family and prison guards, he was the only person allowed to see Susan in the flesh, and the only one permitted to talk to her at length. Prosecutor Tommy Pope fretted that this was all part of a scheme to enroll Susan in a crash program at David Bruck's "insanity school." He became even more certain of it when Bruck dropped strong hints that Susan's mental health wasn't all it seemed.

"People are more complicated than what you can put together out of the bits and pieces of their life," Bruck said.

Bruck was good at the sympathy game. He had to be. For a man who'd devoted his entire career to saving the despised from death, David Bruck intuited that eliciting pity was the only thing in the world that might save Susan Smith's life.

But with the quickie indictments in place, and public sentiment still resoundingly against his client, would pity be enough? The prosecution takes Round Two, on points.

22

Who Are You Calling Crazy?

Love truth, but pardon error.
He who is merely just is severe.

—Voltaire, *Letter to Frederick the Great,* 1740.

Is Susan Smith certifiably nuts? The answer is as subjective and unpredictable as the opinions of twelve jurors locked into a roomful of psychiatrists—further tilted by the prevailing winds of political discourse. Fellowship among the ranks of the insane is not determined by one constant set of rules. However, the frenetic efforts of Susan's lawyer to keep his client in shrink-free territory speaks volumes about the diagnoses some top mental health professionals, experts in the field of child-killing, are likely to impart.

One such expert is Dr. Lee Leifer, whose work has led him through the minds of mothers and fathers who have shot, drowned, bludgeoned, and mutilated their children. From his observation of the Smith case, Dr. Leifer's considered opinion is of the type that would keep David Bruck up at night.

His bottom line: Susan Smith is no psychopath.

Dr. Leifer, an assistant clinical professor of psychiatry at Columbia Medical School of Physicians and Surgeons in New York, is also an attending psychiatrist at St. Vincent's Medical Center. He spent seventeen years as director of a medical and outpatient drug-treatment center, which brought the doctor into contact with thousands of patients whose cases bear similarities to that of Susan Smith. Whether they are insane, in a technical sense, is a matter to be decided by the criminal justice system. But it is up to people like Dr. Leifer to help navigate the bumpy road that so often obscures a court's arrival at a clear-headed opinion as to whether parents who kill their children are legally responsible for their actions.

Dr. Leifer believes the mental state exhibited by Susan Smith places the young mother into a category known as "impulse-control disorder"—a form of borderline personality disorder. The disorder is marked by the drastic means Susan chose for acquiring the things she wanted—actions made easier by her inability to feel empathy for the little ones she felt she needed to get out of her way.

After the murders, Susan, fully cognizant of the consequences of her crime, made a display of remorse. But while technically aware of the difference between right and wrong—the key thing that sets Susan apart from the true psychopath—the person with borderline personality disorder has a gift for rationalizing away the damage she inflicts. That is because she lacks the ordinary person's ability to feel the pain of others. This lack of empathy can grow out of repeated rejection.

"The statements that she made show she wanted to get back with this guy, Tom Findlay, who rejected her," says Leifer. People with impulse-control disorder are typically "raised early in life with a deficiency of fathering and mothering. Susan's father committed suicide, abandoned her. Then her mother remarried.

"A mother who is trying to get close to her new husband not uncommonly may push aside her daughter. We can speculate that there was an insufficiency of maternal nurturing."

Some of Susan's emotional patterns may have resulted from her attempts to follow her mother's example. "She had her mother as a role model: She has intense relationships that end, then she moves on."

Leifer says a common thread that runs through most impulse-control disorder patients is "not only the fact that there appears to be a deficiency of both paternal and maternal nurturing, but also a lack of sibling nurturing." Susan's closest sibling, her brother, Scotty, is nine years her senior; through much of Susan's young life, Scotty was married and busy raising his own family.

"Such a person deprived of that nurturing builds up tremendous reserves of anger and rage, which burden this person all through her life, and at times that rage breaks through," the psychiatrist explains. "That's why you have borderline people who commit tremendous amounts of violence and destruction in this world."

Curiously, the way society looks at antisocial personalities has changed radically with the times. Many politicians, influenced by shrinks, no longer seem willing to believe that some people just don't belong in society—or are just plain bad. As the saying goes: Crime is everyone's fault, but no one is responsible. Years ago, people who were unable or unwilling to follow societal rules were treated as psychiatric cases or thrown in jail. Today, the rush is on to excuse even the most brutal behavior by faulting the culture in which the felon lives.

In the cloistered world of the courtroom, public outrage against crime plays less of a role than ever before in American history. Leifer explains why:

"I had a woman who told me she murdered five people, including her friend's child," Leifer says. "Why? She didn't use excuses like middle-class people—'I was drunk, I was out of my mind.' She said, 'They were in my way. They didn't give me what I needed.'" In extreme cases like this one, explains Leifer, patients, either through mental disorder or hideous upbringing, fail to develop any sort of conscience. "In psychiatry that's called psychopathic personality disorder—they're psychopaths." In this day and age, however, society is frozen in the presence of the psychopath.

"They confound courts, do-gooders, and judges," says Leifer. "A sadist shows no remorse. They don't feel anything for the rights of others.

"People who used to be psychiatric cases are now considered to be people who emulate many of our stars—rap stars who break guitars and rape women," says Leifer. "These have become role models for a certain number of youths. Before, they were considered disturbed. Now, they're considered victims of society."

Now for the backlash. Social theorists recently have started to decry what they see as a tendency, growing out of middle-class guilt, to coddle criminals.

U.S. Senator Daniel Patrick Moynihan, D-New York, has given a name to the increasing institutional tolerance awarded sociopaths and criminals that he believes chips away at the overall quality of life— "Defining deviancy down."

With fingers being pointed everywhere, except at the criminal, law and order has never been so difficult to enforce, deviant behavior so hard to define. Meanwhile, violence continues apace.

"If you have a borderline personality disorder being formed, you have a person with a tremendous amount of rage and a hunger for closeness and attachment that is unfulfilled," explains Dr. Leifer. "Therefore, this person, when she attaches herself to somebody, never finds that this person lives up to her expectations." Susan, according to Leifer, apparently tried to substitute a parent's unconditional love with the immature affections of David, then later, Tom Findlay.

"She's trying to find in this person the missed father and mother she never had." When her needs aren't met "she gets enraged and breaks it off." In other words, she has short, intense relationships that are doomed from the start.

"There was her husband," the doctor continues. "You don't know about all the other guys in her past. Another characteristic of this disorder is the inability to handle all the anger that's piled up inside her."

And that's when the sweet-faced woman turns truly scary.

"Yet another characteristic is, because she missed this early nurturing, she formed a very poor sense of self-identity. That's why such people used to be called 'as-if' personalities." Such people behave "as-if" they are anything other than who they really are.

"If they take on a role," Leifer explains, "they make wonderful actors and actresses."

To many, the most perplexing aspect of Susan's crime was the convincing manner in which she lied about the murders for nine days. To a man who has worked with hundreds of people who share Susan's ability to tell the wildest tales as if they had lived those experiences, this strange scenario is but another component of a familiar psychiatric profile.

"People on stage whom I've treated as a psychoanalyst say, 'When I'm playing a role, I feel as if I'm that person. When I'm not playing a role, I don't know who I am.'

"Think of this woman and the role she played after the murders, the role of the aggrieved mother, begging, making up a story of a black man who attacked her. The beautiful act she put on. She was playing the 'as-if' aggrieved mother, the mother despondent over the kidnapping of her children."

But all the fancy psychiatric texts in all the libraries on the planet can't excuse the fact that an accomplished actress rehearses her role before taking the stage. Susan planned her performance—even if she accepted the role at the last minute. She knew exactly what she was playing at.

"This is not a psychotic disturbance," explains Leifer. "It's premeditated what she did. This is not a dissociative personality. She had to have [the killings] in mind when she went out there to the lake. She was protecting herself by saying she was really going there to kill herself.

"She was able to carry on another premeditated act"—inventing lies about the carjacker—"after the deaths of her children. This is not a thinking disorder." And that is another thing that separates Susan's actions from those of the candidate for the proverbial rubber room.

"A psychotic couldn't do this."

A close reading of the literature provides nothing to get Susan off the hook. While her actions cannot be construed as "normal" by most of us, there was a definite method to her madness.

"My opinion, based on what she said, 'I felt I couldn't be a good mom anymore—I'm the wrong mother for these children, they wouldn't grow up well with the kind of person I am.' It shows she has no positive feeling toward these children, or for herself being worthwhile as a mother. They were in the way.

"A borderline has to get attached to somebody, will do anything to get to that person. Also, she is very attention-getting. She tries to get attention from the person who rejected her. A borderline is so self-involved, she has no compassion for anybody else. She would reason this way: 'I could get [Findlay] back, since he said he didn't want to be a father, by getting rid of the children. Then, I would be a woman whom he could not reject.'"

Relinquishing custody of Michael and Alex to Susan's mother or to David Smith were not realistic options in Susan's quest for a new life. "She would have to stay attached to them, do things for them. They would still be in the way," says Leifer. Still, Susan's reasons for killing the boys were more involved than a simple yen for convenience.

"The self-hatred she has is projected on the children. She hates herself, and the children were just an extension of herself. She did not see them as separate objects. So, the choice was either to kill herself, or them."

But Susan made her choice long before she rolled up to the lake, Leifer believes.

"What was more important than anything was her attachment to the boyfriend who didn't want her.

That was her single focus. So instead of murdering herself through suicide, she got rid of the children."

The logic is nightmarish: Susan Smith decided she had to kill her children so that she would not have to kill herself.

"The borderline must reattach herself to some object. She will do *anything* to be attached. It doesn't matter what she does to get attention of the one who doesn't want her.

"Another characteristic of borderlines is they feel dead inside. They can't stimulate themselves. That's why so many of them get addicted to drugs."

Leifer believes it's always a good idea for authorities to perform drug tests on suspected felons. However, nine days had passed between the commission of Susan's crime and her confession—longer than most drugs tend to stay in the system. Besides, Susan has no known history of drug abuse, except for a couple of brushes with aspirin. In any case, courts no longer accept drug or alcohol abuse as factors that mitigate against a defendant's guilt in the commission of violent crime. Drug abuse is one abuse-excuse that's been stricken from the books.

Leifer seriously doubts Susan's earlier flirtations with suicide were genuine attempts on her life. "When a suicide attempt is real, you do it and don't let anyone know. When it's an attention-getting device, you let someone know right away so they can save you.

"This is part of the borderline personality—a perfect example." Borderline personalities use histrionics, anything that's necessary, to grab the undivided attention of others in an attempt to replace their own missing feelings of self-worth.

"She acts bigger than life," says Leifer. "Her whole life is an act."

But even the best act can wear thin. "The hunger for attention is so great, such people finally confess to get more attention."

While so many in our culture consider a mother killing her own children to be an unnatural act, Leifer has learned that women are not born with the nurturing instinct—what he calls the "American myth of what it takes to be a mother."

"Women are not born with any more love for children than a man is," he says. Love is a feeling that is learned. Or so we hope.

"I've had hundreds of women patients with five or ten children. Why do they have them? You hear the same answers all the time: 'I've never had anything from my mother, my father I never knew. Now, I have something all my own for a short while.' Then the baby gets older."

Short, intense, and satisfying relationships, to these kinds of mothers, come with built-in expiration dates. "These women feel they have nothing and have nobody. All they do is get pregnant."

People who work with violent mothers point out that, in many cases, the women let off signals—sometimes for years—warning about the disaster to come. Often, the mothers have been psychiatric patients or clients of social-services agencies. But governments are notoriously ill-equipped in dealing effectively with such a deep-rooted social problem. In addition, most municipalities aim their social programs at keeping families intact, rather than tearing them apart. Mistakes, of course, are made, often with horrifying consequences. How can you tell with any kind of certainty which mother is about to snap?

According to mental-health experts, however, psychotic mothers can make excellent psychiatric progress, with the help of intensive therapy. The problem is, help often comes along too late to prevent a crime.

In one particularly lurid case, a divorced Ohio mother named Lorene Smith—no relation to the Smiths of South Carolina—apparently suffocated her sons, Michael and Jordan Arno, ages five and three, on Christmas Day 1986. Doctors treating Smith reported in a court-ordered psychiatric evaluation that Lorene Smith believed Christ told her to kill herself and her sons so they could join him in heaven. Like Susan Smith, she carried out only two-thirds of her imagined order.

For two weeks, Smith stayed in the house with her dead sons tucked in their beds, wearing their pajamas. Smith was watching TV when cops broke down the door. The extensive decomposition of their bodies made it impossible for the medical examiner to rule definitively on the boys' cause of death.

Lorene Smith was sentenced to a mental hospital. After six years, psychiatrists were so enthusiastic about her recovery, they recommended her release. She's spent the last two years living with her father, and has exhibited no further violent tendencies.

How do you cure a mother *before* she murders the kids?

Susan Smith did not show psychotic tendencies. And, unlike the many mothers who are watched by social-services personnel, there was no indication Susan was under extreme stress or was prone to violence. In every apparent way, she was the epitome of the perfect mother.

Was Susan Smith crazy or merely calculating? That, of course, is a matter of opinion. Only one thing is absolutely certain: She was one good actress. That is one trait that's hard to cure.

23
Closure

Only a fool would stand in the way of progress.

—Captain Kirk, facing his replacement with a
computer in an episode of *Star Trek*, 1968.

As the year drew toward its conclusion, great news
zapped through town like a badly needed shot in the
arm—Union was getting its first movie theater. And a
multiplex, at that!

For the first time since the city was founded, an
investor—this one a twenty-four-year-old visionary—
put together a deal bound to improve Union's standing as a destination for a Saturday night date. Plans
were in the works to build a six-screen theater
designed to show first-run Hollywood films in a
vacant building in the nearly empty Westgate shopping center, near the Hickory Nuts sports bar. No
more driving thirty miles to Spartanburg to catch a

flick. No more waiting for a film to turn up on satellite TV. Better late than never, Union County chugged along into the twentieth century.

Of course, there were those around town who saw the theater as representing the further diminishment of the church as the focal point of Union's social life. First, a bar. Now, movies. What's next, they wondered, a bowling alley?

But once you set the wheels of progress in motion, there's no turning back. Union, in spite of itself, was on its way. The efforts of people like Mac Johnston, recruited the previous spring to head the local Chamber of Commerce, were paying off handsomely. Under Johnston's direction, Union had waged an aggressive campaign to woo new business, and four plants were now setting up shop in the county. Fresh money always brings fresh blood along with it, and the new faces destined to pop up in town would arrive expecting a few basic amenities, like movies.

The buzz of new industry couldn't have come at a better time; Union was about to lose yet another textile plant. In late 1994, United Merchants announced that it was closing its huge mill in Union, throwing 586 people out of work. Sixty percent of the soon-to-be unemployed were black—a group already plagued with the area's highest unemployment and poverty rates. Many displaced workers were in their forties and fifties, and had worked in textiles their entire adult lives. With cheaper men and women in their late teens and twenties competing for the same jobs, their futures were suddenly in jeopardy.

After all Union had been through, good news was in order. So in early December, Carroll Campbell, South Carolina's outgoing Republican governor, paid a call on the town. Campbell, compelled by his state's term limits to step down after eight years in office, had just accepted a job in Washington as a lobbyist for the National Association of Life Insurance, at a major salary. One of his last acts as governor was to accompany South Carolina's incoming Republican governor, David Beasley, thirty-seven, to a desolate little corner of their mutual home state.

About 200 people turned out at the Union County courthouse to greet the luminaries. Campbell and Beasley took pleasure in telling the downtrodden populace that Union was to be the site of two new textile plants, as well as two new machinery concerns. Jobs galore! News of Union's suddenly improved economic picture was almost as big as that of the town's soon-to-be movie theater, and every bit as welcome.

The mood in the courthouse was festive as the muckety-mucks paid homage to their rural brothers and sisters. Handshaking and picture snapping were the order of the day. But while everyone in the room knew that the men made this trip, at least in part, to soothe battered spirits after Union's recent high-profile torment, the name Susan Smith went unspoken.

Just as four new businesses arrived in the nick of time to replace Union's lost textile plant, new, heinous crimes came along to absorb local attention away from the Susan Smith case. In mid-December, a sixteen-year-old girl, apparently in the process of breaking up with her twenty-one-year-old boyfriend, was shot in the head and killed. The boyfriend was thrown in jail, charged with the young girl's murder. This couple was black.

Soon afterward, Union's courthouse was the scene of a murder trial—a rare event in this part of the state. Gina Riddle, thirty-three, was charged with shooting to death her husband, Mike, with a .357 Magnum in November 1993. Mike, thirty-two, was a wealthy landowner who raised cattle. Each had children from previous marriages. "They were white and pretty," remarked Mac Johnston. In the pre–Susan Smith days, the Riddle killing was considered the most scandalous event to hit Union County in years.

In the trial, held two weeks before Christmas, Gina Riddle testified that Mike had beaten her severely since the first day of their marriage. Evidence was introduced showing that on his last night alive, Mike broke Gina's nose and bashed in her face. When she shot him, Gina testified, her husband was lunging for her again.

The prosecution did a commendable job proving that Gina Riddle had no choice but to kill. The jury found Gina Riddle innocent; the shooting was in self-defense.

Union's homicidal triple-header sent a message to the townsfolk. After Susan Smith's confession to murder, the killing of the teenage girl, and Gina Riddle's acquittal, there was no denying the sad truth that rules domestic affairs, not only in Union County, but just about everywhere: You have more to fear from a person you love than from any stranger who might be lurking in the bushes.

In fact, the only recent murder that anyone in the county believed may have been committed by a stranger occurred back in 1991. A traveling salesman, passing about seven miles outside the city of Union, was stabbed to death in an apparent robbery. Two black men were charged with crime, and both pleaded innocent. At trial, a jury found one of the men not guilty, and he was set free. As for the other defendant, the jury could not decide on a verdict, and the panel deadlocked. By the end of 1994, a new trial had yet to be scheduled. The identity of the salesman's killer or killers was considered a local mystery, but the odd case of the dead stranger didn't prevent anyone from sleeping at night. Many folks simply assumed the true murderer was long gone. The woods, they were certain, were free from peril.

A far more typical example of murder, Union-style, occurred in January 1992, when Carl Mason Maness, a forty-year-old white man, came home to find his wife, Janice, reading a Bugs Bunny story to the couple's child. Apparently convinced his wife was trying to put the devil in the youngster, Maness shot Janice in the head with a .22-caliber rifle. He was tried for murder in May 1992. Carl Maness was found guilty, but mentally ill, and he was sentenced to a mental institution.

In these parts, domestic killings don't usually result in prison sentences, that is, if they result in convictions at all. The last person to be sent to prison for homicide was Lisa Spencer, a white woman who in December 1990 shot and killed her common-law husband, Bobby Eugene Canupp, also white, with a 12-gauge shotgun. As in the case of Gina Riddle, there was evidence of physical abuse in the Spencer-Canupp household. But Lisa Spencer chose not to take her chances before a jury, and pleaded guilty to a reduced charge of voluntary manslaughter. She was sentenced to twelve years in prison.

Keeping homicide in the family may be the custom in Union, but Susan Smith was different. You just don't kill your kids—folks tend to frown on that sort of thing. However hard she worked to make herself look like the devoted mother and perfect citizen, Union had never seen the likes of Susan Smith. And they hoped they'd never see anything like her again.

*   *   *

An odd thing happened in December. Donations started trickling in to Union from around the country.

It started after Union County Supervisor Dale Robinson worried publicly that the county might not be able to afford Susan Smith's trial, which was expected to commence the following spring. The entire budget for the 16th Circuit court system contained just $60,000 for such things as expert witness fees. Should Susan Smith's trial cost half a million or a million dollars—not unreasonable in a high-profile murder case with an aggressive defense lawyer—Robinson said, in effect, "We're screwed."

Suddenly, the checks started coming. A few dollars from Georgia. Some more from Mississippi. Some folks in Bosworth, Montana, pitched in and sent $270 to Union. "From a little town that cares," read the attached note.

It was too much. Robinson and Solicitor Tommy Pope appeared on *Larry King Live*—this time, urging people to save their money. But the loot arrived in tiny chunks, eventually totaling some $500. Union officials put it aside, just in case. Then Union turned the subject of conversation away from Susan Smith. It was time for life to return, more or less, to normal.

David Smith's father and stepmother eventually left David's apartment, and returned to California, leaving him alone with his memories. Twice, David's mother, Barbara Benson, drove to Union along with her older son, David's half-brother, Bill Kull. It wasn't easy for the grandmother, but someone had to sleep in little Michael's bed, a well-designed piece of furniture that converted easily into an adult-sized double bed.

"I'm doing all right. Everything's fine." David

protested so fervently to his relatives, he made it impossible for anyone to argue. By this time, he'd gone back at work at Winn-Dixie. But something about him just wasn't the same.

"He's still in a state of shock," Bill Kull, twenty-eight, believes.

"He's trying to get back to normal. He's taking it one day at a time. He's still trying to understand why this happened."

At Christmastime, without telling anyone, David skipped town and went to stay in California with his mother and stepfather. The prospect of spending the holidays without his wife and children was too terrible. Union was filled with too many ghosts.

Susan Smith spent Christmas and New Year's exactly as she spent Thanksgiving—behind bars, staring at the photographs of the children she killed. Each day, the life she threw away, the streets of the town she may never again walk, the faces of people she may never see again, loomed larger in her mind.

The feeling was not mutual.

As the churches celebrated the birth of their Lord, the citizens of Union set about the task of getting back to business as usual. As quickly as Susan Smith had torn them down, the townsfolk again erected barriers against prying eyes. They closed the shutters around their sins, and erected warm smiles over their pain. Once again, their secrets were safe.

As the days passed, the name Susan Smith turned into a dirty word, never spoken in public. Her face faded from the town's consciousness as abruptly as it entered.

Winter arrived in Union, forcing the leaves off the trees. But the days were still balmy, the nights as quiet and dull as always. Life really hadn't changed much at all.

In time, even the blue and black ribbons, memorials to Michael and Alex, came down from the homes. Pictures of the boys, not long ago pinned to every breast, were stashed in drawers and out of sight. Even the newspapers, once crammed with stories about Susan's crime, stuck new developments on progressively deeper pages. Eventually, the saga of Susan Smith fell out of the papers entirely.

It couldn't last. Soon, there would be a trial. The reporters would return. Union's wounds would be opened anew. But for the time being, the town did everything it could to exorcise the demon mother from its midst.

Says Mac Johnston: "It's like the whole thing never even happened."

Epilogue

By mid-January 1995, Prosecutor Tommy Pope arrived at the decision the entire nation had been waiting to hear: Pope said he'd seek to have Susan Smith put to death in South Carolina's electric chair if convicted.

In making the difficult call, Pope had help from none other than David Smith. After more than two months of grieving, David was finally ready to let go of his wife. David let it be known that he welcomed Susan's execution.

In December, David Smith made the seventy-mile drive to Columbia for a face-to-face meeting with his wife.

Susan Smith was led in chains into the visitor's room where David waited, and her bonds were removed. As guards stood by, the inmate took a seat across the table from her husband. Throughout their brief conversation, Susan was unable to meet David's steely gaze.

David stared emotionlessly into the face of the woman he loved, clad in her blue prison uniform, that familiar ponytail on top of her head. Susan had lost weight. She was paler than before, and she wore no makeup. Otherwise, Susan hadn't changed one bit.

The meeting was restrained. Since she was taken off suicide watch, Susan was careful never to shed tears in the presence of guards, out of fear they would again deem her suicidal, confiscate her meager possessions, and put her back in that dreaded paper gown. David wasn't in any mood for high drama, either. He never really was the type who went in for that sort of thing.

With the court case pending, David understood that this was not the time to demand any explanations from Susan. Instead, he requested this meeting to discuss some business matters outstanding between two people undergoing a divorce. Such as— What should we do about the house? David wanted to keep the little nest on Toney Road, but it remained in his wife's legal possession.

They never did talk about Michael and Alex.

As of this writing, Susan Vaughan Smith, indicted on two counts of first-degree murder in the drowning deaths of her children, Michael Daniel Smith, age three, and Alexander Tyler Smith, fourteen months, has yet to stand trial. Her defense lawyer, David Bruck, has delayed announcing whether he will seek an insanity defense in South Carolina's most notorious murder case. Despite strenuous protests by Solicitor Tommy Pope, Bruck's move has guaranteed Susan Smith at least three months in jail without being compelled to undergo an examination by an independent psychiatrist.

Union County's finances, which could be strained beyond its limits by a lengthy murder trial, may get some relief from the massive publicity the case has generated. With all the scorn heaped on Susan by the citizens of Union, Bruck is believed to have an excellent chance, if he so wishes, to secure a change of venue for a trial. The challenge will be finding any place where twelve men and women exist who have never heard the name Susan Smith.

Susan continues to spend twenty-three hours a day in a six-by-fourteen-foot cell, painted beige and brown, in the administrative segregation unit of the Women's Correctional Center in Columbia, South Carolina. For one hour a day, she is allowed to roam the sunlit confines of a tiny, cement-floored exercise yard. Susan's cell, furnished with a bunk, sink, and toilet, is located in a wing that sits just a few hundred feet from the state's electric chair. Susan was placed in the high-security unit for her own protection against those who wish her harm, who still number many. South Carolina has not executed a woman since 1947.

The inmate continues to receive weekly visits from her mother and stepfather, Linda and Beverly Russell. Her husband, David, has come to see her just once.

Michael and Alex Smith lie in peace in a family plot at the Bogansville United Methodist Church, outside the city of Union, next to David Smith's brother, Daniel. Since their murders, mothers and fathers around the nation have continued killing their own flesh and blood at more or less the same rate as before. However, officials at such child-saving organizations as the National Center for Missing and Exploited Children in Arlington, Virginia, report that the Susan Smith case has caused a dramatic increase in awareness of the plight of the nation's most vulnerable citizens. In the end, the best thing that might come out of this senseless tragedy is that another young life will be spared because of it.

Andrea Peyser is a columnist for the *New York Post*.
She lives in Brooklyn, New York.